Escape
Domestic
Violence

Helen Grant
Edited by Denise Robertson

KT-164-378

 GRANADA

Ventures

 This
Morning

Hodder Arnold

A MEMBER OF THE HODDER HEADLINE GROUP

Orders: Please contact Bookpoint Ltd, 130 Milton Park, Abingdon
Oxon OX14 4SB. Telephone: (44) 01235 827720. Fax: (44) 01235
400454. Lines are open 09.00 to 5.00, Monday to Saturday, with a 24-
hour message answering service. You can also order through our
website www.hoddereducation.co.uk.

British Library Cataloguing in Publication Data
A catalogue record for this title is available from the British Library.

ISBN-13: 978 0 340 94322 9

First published   2007
Impression number 10 9 8 7 6 5 4 3 2 1
Year   2012 2011 2010 2009 2008 2007

Typeset by Transet Limited, Coventry, England.
Printed in Great Britain for Hodder Education, a division of Hodder
Headline, an Hachette Livre UK Company, 338 Euston Road, London,
NW1 3BH, by Cox & Wyman Ltd, Reading, Berkshire.

Hodder Headline's policy is to use papers that are natural, renewable
and recyclable products and made from wood grown in sustainable
forests. The logging and manufacturing processes are expected to
conform to the environmental regulations of the country of origin.

ABOUT THE AUTHORS

Helen Grant has been a writer and journalist since 1998. She is the founder and editor of *H* – an online magazine for media, creative and showbiz talent, and in 2007 she launched the networking website myhezine.com. Helen has written articles for several women's magazines, including *Grazia, She, Real, Prima, Love it, Junior* and *Mother & Baby* as well as a number of articles for teenage magazines and international publications.

Denise Robertson's television career began with BBC *Breakfast Time* in 1984. She has been the resident agony aunt of ITV's *This Morning* for the last 20 years. In that time, she has received over 200,000 letters covering a wide range of problems from viewers and readers of her newspaper and magazine columns. She has written 19 novels and several works of non-fiction. Her autobiography, *Agony: Don't Get Me Started*, was published in paperback by Little Books in July 2007. She is associated with many charities, among them Relate, The Bubble Foundation, Careline and the National Council for the Divorced and Separated.

WHICH PAGE?

What should I do in an emergency? *Turn to pages 87 and 124*

I think someone I know is being abused. What can I do? *Turn to pages 77 and 263*

I'm ready to leave my abuser. How can I do it? *Turn to page 199*

What is a refuge? *Turn to page 211*

Are men abused or is it just women? *Turn to pages 20 and 151*

Can the legal system help me? *Turn to page 223*

My children are suffering from the situation at home. What can I do? *Turn to pages 70 and 237*

I have lost my self-confidence. Is there anything that will help? *Turn to page 253*

Which organizations can help me? *Turn to page 307*

This book is dedicated to my children Louise, Abigail and Callum for the love and laughter they have brought into my life. It is also dedicated to the many people worldwide who are suffering the heartache and pain of domestic violence. Always remember that you are not alone.

I would like to thank my agent, Liz Puttick, for giving me the opportunity to write this book and, in doing so, launch my career as an author.

I would like to thank Victoria Roddam for having faith in my abilities as a writer, for overseeing the project and helping to shape it, and for her much appreciated advice.

I would like to thank my husband Colin for the endless mugs of tea during late nights of research, and for his love and patience.

I would also like to thank Denise Pfeiffer for her support, encouragement and enthusiasm; Russ King for his cheerful emails; and my sister Lynsey for the late night chats.

I would like to thank my mother, father and grandmother for supporting me so steadfastly throughout this project and for being my most devoted fans.

Finally, I would like to pay tribute to my grandfather, who I miss dearly. I sense his presence every day.

Helen Grant, 2007

CONTENTS

FOREWORD

By Fern Britton and Phillip Schofield

As presenters of ITV's *This Morning*, over many years we have met many incredible people with many incredible stories to tell. What we have learnt is that life can be wonderful but it can also be very hard.

Our phone-ins have generated thousands of calls a day from viewers all over Great Britain looking for suitable advice on a range of subjects. What is very obvious from these calls is that we are not alone with the personal challenges we often face and there is a great need for help in dealing with them. We are always cheered by the follow-up letters and emails from viewers saying how our experts' advice has helped them to turn their lives around.

Over the 20 years *This Morning* has been on air, Denise Robertson, our agony aunt, has regularly offered support and advice to millions of viewers on a huge range of personal problems and she spends even more time off-screen answering letters, calling those in distress and dealing with questions via the internet. As a result she is uniquely qualified to edit these books which reflect the common sense and sensitive advice that we provide on the show.

We believe these survival guides will help you to deal with the practical and emotional fallout caused by issues such as bereavement, relationship break-ups, debt, infertility, addiction, domestic violence and depression.

If you feel that your particular problems are insurmountable – don't! There is always a way to improve your life or at least get yourself on a path towards a new start. If you think you are alone with your problem – don't! Our experience shows that many of us face the same problems but are often reluctant to admit it. You have already made a great start by picking up this book.

We both wish you all the strength and support you need to tackle your own personal problems and sincerely hope that we can help through these books and through our continued work on the programme.

INTRODUCTION

I vividly remember the first victim of domestic violence I interviewed. She was sitting opposite me in a radio studio, wearing a surgical collar as a result of her husband throwing her down the stairs. 'How long did the abuse go on?' I asked. She answered 'Eight years', and I was suddenly lost for words. How could anyone endure such treatment for eight days, let alone eight years? In those early days, my ignorance meant that I saw easy solutions to the problem. Someone hit you and you left them, never to return. It took years and the patience and friendship of victims to help me understand the complexities of the domestic violence situation. I needed to grasp how intelligent women, and a smaller number of men, can be slowly broken down until they may even come to believe that they deserve punishment and that, somehow, their partner's violence is their fault.

Often the abuser will say 'You drove me to this', as though there could ever be a justification for vileness. Now I understand the fears that may lie behind a victim's reluctance to flee the abuse.

In spite of the fact that help is available and there are laws to secure their rights, they still write to tell me they fear being homeless or deprived of their children – or perhaps subjected to even worse violence than that which they have escaped. 'I'll kill you if you go' is a threat all too easy to believe if you are already battered into submission.

Physical violence is not the only form of abuse. The letters I have received that tell of emotional abuse are just as harrowing to read. The gradual shutting out of friends and family, the constant criticism of appearance or abilities, the verbal assaults that instil such fear that you become afraid to function. One woman told me of her desperation each morning as she tried to time his boiled egg to the right consistency to avoid a tongue-lashing. Strangely, no matter how hard she tried, it was never 'just right'. The egg ritual was his little bit of pleasure before he left for work.

In the last few years we have realized that abuse can also happen in same-sex relationships and to the elderly, sometimes with devastating results. This book is written for all sufferers, and those who care about them, in the hope that it will help them navigate to happier waters.

Denise Robertson

Part 1:
What to Do
Right Now

The information, support and guidance in this book is for *anyone* whose life has been affected by domestic violence and abuse – whether male or female, adult, child or the elderly, heterosexual or those in same-sex relationships – regardless of your gender, age, ethnic background or sexual orientation. It is also for anyone supporting or caring for a person who they suspect – or already know – is suffering domestic abuse. Throughout the book, we refer to the abuser as 'he' because in most reported cases of domestic violence the male is the abuser. However, we are very much aware that men can also be victims so regardless of the terms we use, the information in this book is for anyone who is suffering abuse, male or female. Male victims will find Part 3 especially helpful as it deals specifically with violence towards men.

After you have read Part 1, you will be more aware of whether or not you have been abused, and what sort of abuse you are suffering. You'll find some help about the difficult feelings, some early advice about leaving, and you will have a clear understanding of domestic abuse. You can then start to think about your options, and begin to support yourself and your children through the times ahead – or support your friend or relative, if you suspect they are being abused.

By the end of Part 1 you will:

- Know what domestic abuse is

- Know what signs to look out for

- Be able to tell the difference between different types of abuse

- Understand how domestic abuse affects you and your children.

1

What is domestic abuse?

Help

The national 24-hour free domestic violence helpline number in the UK is 0808 2000 247. This is repeated in the resources section in Part 6. Call this number if you are feeling scared, anxious or confused about your situation. Someone who understands exactly what you are going through will answer your call and offer you practical and emotional support. If you are an elderly person, you can also call the Action On Elder Abuse helpline on 0808 808 8141. A helpful point of contact for male victims is the Men's Advice Line (MALE) on 0845 064 6800. Gay or lesbian victims can call Broken Rainbow on 08452 60 44 60 or the London Lesbian and Gay Switchboard on 020 7837 7324.

In loving relationships, people respect each other's needs. They don't hit, slap, punch or kick the person they claim to love. They don't threaten violence and they don't make their loved one feel insignificant, humiliated and controlled. Are you afraid of your partner or a loved one? Does he lose his temper and then blame you for provoking him? Has he threatened to harm you, your children or other family members? Does he say things like, 'If you shaped up, I wouldn't have to knock you around'? Have you stopped seeing your friends and family in case it makes your partner angry?

If you answered yes to any of the above, you are being abused. What your abuser is doing has nothing to do with love. It is about power and control. He might blame you for his behaviour but really the abuse has nothing to do with you and everything to do with him and his extreme jealousy, insecurity, difficulty managing anger and traditional beliefs about how men and women should act. **Please don't think that you are to blame in any way.** You do not 'belong' to him. You are your own person and do not deserve to be treated with violence and contempt regardless of what you may or may not have done. There is no excuse for violence or abuse – *ever*.

Domestic abuse is not always between a husband and wife. It can happen in any type of relationship including mother and daughter, father and daughter, mother and son, father and son, brother and sister, boyfriend and girlfriend and same-sex relationships. If the abuse is taking place within your family or an intimate relationship, it is domestic abuse. **All domestic abuse is wrong.**

In this part of the book, we will help you to understand what is happening to you and begin to give you back a sense of control by providing you with the knowledge of what domestic abuse is. Just knowing what is happening is a step towards change. In Part 5, we share with you the experiences of others, who felt what you are feeling now. Hopefully their stories will make you feel less alone.

Let's start by looking at what you absolutely *must* do in an emergency.

- Call 999 or your local police station. Tell them you need help immediately.

- Encourage your children to get out of the house and get help.

- If you have a safety alarm or mobile phone, use it to alert the emergency services.

- If you can't get to a phone, try to alert a neighbour or passer-by.

- Stay away from areas where there are potential weapons, such as the kitchen, bathroom or garden.

- Scream, shout, bang on walls or a window, and make as much noise as possible.

- If you or the children have been badly hurt, call 999 and ask for an ambulance.

Above all, make you and your children your immediate priority and do whatever it takes to protect yourself and them. If you sense a violent episode is about to occur, get out of the house before things get any worse. Don't argue with your abuser. It's pointless and won't get you anywhere because the only opinion he is interested in is his own. Do whatever you can to distance yourself from him and try to lessen the tension by staying calm. If you can't leave the house, move into another room, remembering to avoid areas where there are potential weapons – and **please tell someone what is happening**.

Call your mum, dad, best friend, a neighbour or anyone else you trust and can rely on for help.

Remember, **none of this is your fault**, despite what he may say. You probably feel really alone right now but please be assured you are not. There are support networks on hand who will do everything they can to help. There is so much you can do to help make your life better and so many people who can help you make some much-needed changes. Now let's begin to look at what domestic abuse is.

Q. What is domestic abuse?

A. Domestic abuse is when one person in a marriage or intimate relationship tries to control the other person. The abuser uses fear and intimidation and may threaten to use or actually use physical violence. Domestic abuse that includes physical violence is called domestic violence.

How to recognize domestic abuse

Domestic abuse is rarely a one-off event. It always escalates over time. It usually occurs within a close relationship and it is not always physical. It can be psychological, financial or sexual, or a combination of some, or all, of these. Most victims are women but it happens to men and children too. If you are a man who is being abused by a female partner, you will find Part 3 of this book helpful in terms of gaining an insight into what is happening and feeling less alone. Domestic violence against men is every bit as terrifying, confusing and horrific as violence towards women.

Right now, you are probably feeling emotionally confused, with little or no self-esteem. You may have been told that you are a useless, ugly, fat, waste of space, and a rubbish wife, girlfriend or mother. It is likely that you have come to accept these insults as the truth. If you are constantly being told that you are a stupid, bad person and that you deserve everything you get, you will eventually start believing it. Being made to believe that you are worthless makes it more difficult to think about getting help. So, you might also be feeling trapped, lonely and isolated.

Please believe us when we say that your partner is speaking to you in this way to undermine your confidence. He wants to control you, not just physically but mentally too, and he wants to make you feel so emotionally worthless that you become dependent on him and grateful for the small scraps of pleasure he offers, if any.

When you have finished reading this book, we hope you have enough insight to acknowledge the areas of your life that are no longer working and to make confident, wise changes.

Does your partner make you feel like a horrible person? How confident are you that others find you attractive? Chances are he's told you that no one else will want you and that staying with him is the best offer you'll get. In reality, most domestic violence survivors say that leaving their abuser was the best thing they ever did. They relish their independence and love the fact that they no longer have to answer to anyone. When they enter another relationship, and most do, they continue to value their independence and are stronger, happier and wiser.

Psychological abuse can sometimes be more damaging than physical violence. Having little confidence has the knock-on effect of clouding your judgement, making it difficult to know what to do. It doesn't matter if you are being hit daily or once every three months, the damage to your self-esteem will be the same. You will be walking on eggshells, desperately trying to please and praying that the next beating never comes. Being brutally attacked by the person who claims to love you is the worst kind of betrayal. The misery, fear and isolation that you feel every day are mental scars that last long after the bruises have faded.

If you sense that he may carry out his threats of violence, please tell someone straightaway. If he has attacked you before, perhaps several times, you may feel too embarrassed and ashamed to tell anyone. But most people will understand, and they will want to help. If you are unlucky enough to confide in someone who is judgemental and critical, and it is an unfortunate fact of life that some people are incapable of showing empathy and understanding, please believe that not everyone will respond in such an unhelpful way.

What you are going through is definitely *not* your fault. **No one deserves to be beaten or abused** – physically, mentally, emotionally, financially or sexually – **under any circumstances**. The blame and responsibility for what has happened belong to your abuser and no one else. You have no need to feel ashamed or embarrassed, and you are most definitely not alone. There are many, many people, young and old, feeling the same emotions that you are feeling right now.

MYTH: Domestic abuse doesn't happen to men.

FACT: Most people who experience domestic abuse are women but a significant number of men experience domestic abuse, as do transgender, gay and bisexual males and females.

Q. What are the harmful effects of domestic violence?

A. Victims don't just suffer physical injuries from domestic assaults; they also experience health problems from the stress of living in a violent relationship. Long-term health problems include drug and alcohol abuse, depression, sexually transmitted diseases, seizures, migraines and arthritis as well as post-traumatic stress disorder and problems during pregnancy.

There is a mistaken belief that domestic abuse is about losing control when in fact it is about one person in a relationship deliberately controlling another. For victims, this can be distressing and puzzling, and extremely frightening, and it is equally as terrifying for women who have been in abusive relationships before as for those who are experiencing it for the first time. All abuse hurts.

It doesn't matter if you are a man or a woman, a girl or boy, young or old, or the relationship is heterosexual or same sex, you can be abused in all kinds of relationships and it can start at any time. You may not remember exactly when your abuse began or how, as it may have seemed less obvious at first. Your abuser will have been keen to hide his true nature until your relationship became more established and he was sure of your feelings towards him. Until then, he was probably charming and romantic, maybe excessively so. In his bid to win you over, he would have said what he thought you wanted to hear, displaying the 'nicer' side of his personality and keeping the darker side hidden for later.

Perhaps in your case the abuse started in the early days of your relationship, or maybe it began suddenly after several years. Both are common scenarios. Have you recently broken up with someone and they refuse to accept that the relationship is over? Perhaps your partner has been psychologically and financially abusing you for a long time, and the abuse recently turned physical or sexual. Whatever your circumstances, you will understandably be feeling terrified, vulnerable and confused.

It can take weeks, months or sometimes years for psychological abuse to turn physical. Sometimes it can happen within days. There is no typical timescale but if you are being abused, it will always get worse with time. Your abuser will have become more controlling as your relationship became more 'established' and he felt confident that he had you under his spell.

> *MYTH: Domestic violence is caused by drug and alcohol abuse.*
>
> **FACT:** Heavy drinking and substance abuse can escalate violence but they do not cause it. Many violent episodes occur when a person is sober.

On the other hand, many women who are controlled by their partners have never been physically assaulted, and never will be. Perhaps that is the case for you, but the constant fear that your partner could become violent any day is painful enough. The psychological torture of not knowing what's coming next can be as terrifying as the physical act of violence itself. One of your abuser's favourite tricks is to use fear tactics to control your every move. He may play cat and mouse, toying with your emotions by using mind games to make you feel trouble is just around the corner.

It can be a huge shock to suddenly be confronted with the nasty side of a person who you thought loved you. When you put your trust in someone and they betray you in such a cruel way, the damage runs deep. It may take a long time, if ever, to feel that level of trust for him again. If the relationship ends, there is also a danger of carrying your past experience into future relationships. Learning to trust again will take time and effort.

The violence started almost as soon as he moved in. He would hit me for the slightest thing. If he couldn't think of a reason, he'd hit me anyway.

Linda

Domestic abuse causes far more pain than the visible marks of bruises and scars. It is devastating to be abused by someone that you love and think loves you in return.

Diane Feinstein

What if you are a male victim?

Everyone knows that female victims of domestic violence live in hell, but what if you are a male victim? There are frequent reports of men being assaulted by their current or former partners, sustaining physical injury, or even death. Part 3 focuses on violence towards men, but in the meantime let's begin to look at what it is and how it makes men feel.

Does your partner hit, kick, punch and bite you when she is furious, jealous, frustrated, or high on drugs or alcohol? Does she have problems controlling her temper, throw objects at you, smash up your home, punch doors, destroy your personal possessions or threaten to harm you or your children? Perhaps your partner is jealous and controlling, monitoring your every move and exploding with anger if you so much as glance in the direction of another woman? Or maybe you're in a gay relationship that is controlling. Remember that abuse happens in homosexual relationships as much as it does in heterosexual relationships, and as all abuse tends to follow a pattern, the advice in this book is appropriate for anyone experiencing domestic abuse, regardless of gender, sexual orientation, ethic background or age.

Your partner may make you feel like you are going crazy, playing mind games and manipulating your emotions. Next time she tells you she is acting out of love, remember that abuse is not about love; it is about power and control.

Protecting yourself and your children must be your number one priority. If your wife or girlfriend is abusing you, you may feel reluctant or embarrassed to speak out about what is happening. Fear, shame, confusion and paranoia are normal reactions. Talking to someone who is non-judgemental and sympathetic will help. Part 6 of this book lists some useful numbers for you to call.

Despite the statistics, women are five times more likely than men to report domestic abuse, and domestic violence helplines are primarily geared towards women and children fleeing violence. However, the reality is that domestic violence can happen to men *and* women, so protecting yourself and your children is crucial.

Is there someone you can speak to that you trust? Think about all the people you know and choose someone who is a good listener, sympathetic and non-judgemental. It doesn't have to be a friend or family member. It can be a work colleague, doctor, teacher, priest, your boss, or a neighbour. You can also call one of the domestic violence helplines listed in Part 6 of this book. The person at the end of the phone will offer practical ways to help, and emotional guidance in a sympathetic, caring and non-judgemental way. They will not pressurize you into making decisions that you are not ready for. Domestic violence counsellors are trained professionals who are aware of the realities of abuse and the damage it does to a person's physical and emotional well-being. They are sensitive to the mixed feelings you may have about your abuser and understand that the last thing you want is to be pressured into making a decision.

Q. What does a typical abuser look like?

A. There is no typical abuser. They come from all walks of life, ethnic groups, religion, neighbourhoods and professions. They can be male or female, young or old, heterosexual or homosexual. The majority of perpetrators are men but women can be abusers too.

2

What is psychological and verbal abuse?

Recognizing domestic abuse is not easy, especially when you are living with it every day. Take a look at the following checklist of behaviours which are there to help you decide if you – or someone you know – is being psychologically and verbally abused. Read through the list and tick any that you can identify with.

Does your partner:

❑ Constantly criticize or undermine you?

❑ Call you names?

❑ Put you down in public?

❑ Yell and swear at you?

❑ Criticize your abilities as a wife/girlfriend/mother?

❑ Humiliate and embarrass you in front of others?

❑ Make racial comments towards you?

❑ Behave in an overprotective or extremely jealous manner?

❑ Demand that you spend all your free time with him?

❑ Threaten to hurt or kill you if you don't do what he says?

❑ Have unpredictable mood swings?

❑ Break objects, punch walls and slam doors?

❑ Threaten suicide?

❑ Always make you feel like you are doing the wrong thing?

❑ Watch your every move?

❑ Monitor your phone calls and internet use?

❑ Lock you in the house during the day?

❏ Accuse you of being crazy, paranoid, unfaithful or stupid?

❏ Make you fear for your safety and that of your children?

❏ Threaten to harm or kidnap the children, pets or close family members?

❏ Lose his temper as a way to get you to do what he wants?

❏ Threaten to report you to the police or social services for things you didn't do?

❏ Accuse you of being an unfit mother?

❏ Threaten you with weapons?

❏ Show no sympathy when you are sick or injured?

❏ Refuse to help around the house even when you are pregnant?

❏ Constantly check up on you by phone, email or text?

❏ Make you feel sexually humiliated or under pressure to perform sexual acts that you don't feel comfortable with?

❏ Laugh at you and accuse you of being crazy if you confront him about his behaviour?

❏ Make you feel like you're going crazy?

❏ Play mind games?

How many items on the checklist did you identify with? Some abuse victims will tick one or two, while others may pick almost all of them. As a guide, if you answered yes to two or more of these behaviours you are being psychologically and/or verbally abused. We will now look at what psychological and verbal abuse is like, and how it feels.

Your partner may control your every move, make endless promises and lies, ask constant questions and follow you everywhere, even to the toilet. Or perhaps he limits your independence in other ways, making it difficult for you to see friends and family, disconnecting the phone and hiding your car keys so that you can't use the car.

Does he lose his temper over small, trivial things, call you vicious names and threaten to hurt or kill you, your pets and your children? He may criticize your clothes, make-up, hairstyle or

---

Q: What causes domestic abuse?

A: Domestic abuse starts when one person feels the need to control and dominate another. This is usually due to extreme jealousy, insecurity, low self-esteem, difficulty managing anger or traditional beliefs about how men and women should act.

job, and make it difficult for you to work or refuse to allow you to work at all. Perhaps he locks you in the house and takes the keys to work. These are extreme examples.

Sometimes the abuse can be equally as controlling but in a less obvious way, such as accusing you of having affairs in a 'teasing way' or insisting that you spend all your time together because 'no one else in this world can be trusted.' Do any of these behaviours sound familiar? From the extreme to the mild, they are all a clear indication that you are being psychologically abused. Psychological and verbal abuse are sometimes called emotional abuse.

Another way to tell if you are being abused is to consider the way your partner's actions and words make your feel.

If your partner's actions make you feel depressed, anxious, uncomfortable, angry, scared or upset, there is a chance that you are being psychologically abused. If he shouts, calls you names, criticizes and humiliates you, you are being verbally as well as psychologically abused. Being spoken down to, belittled, made to feel crazy, humiliated, cheap and ugly on a daily basis by someone you choose to spend your life with, or in the case of children have little choice but to, causes all sorts of symptoms that you may or may not have considered connected to the abuse.

There is no way of telling whether the psychological abuse you are suffering will escalate into physical violence but it probably will. He might not hurt you physically or sexually for months or years, and maybe not until the relationship is over, but it *will* get worse unless he seeks help. **Therapy is absolutely crucial**. Without it, there is little or no chance of the violence and abuse stopping.

One of the favourite tools of manipulation in your abuser's weaponry is unpredictability and disproportionate reactions. Does he react with extreme rage to the smallest annoyance, or lie to get his own way, insult and ignore you for his own ends? Perhaps he frightens you by intimidating you, threatening to harm you and your loved ones, threatening to kill, harm pets or

---

MYTH: Battered women provoke abuse.

FACT: Victims do not provoke domestic abuse any more than they do other crimes. Abused women often make repeated attempts to leave violent relationships, but are prevented from doing so by increased violence and control tactics by their abuser.

destroy property. Being attacked with criticism, belittling, name-calling, silent treatment, making and breaking promises and childish tantrums will have undermined your confidence. If you disagree, it may be that your confidence has been damaged in ways that are not immediately apparent. Think back to the person you were before you met your partner – are you still that same person? In what ways have you changed? In Part 4 we look at ways to find the real you again.

Do you feel like you're going crazy sometimes? That's what he wants – for you to believe that you are losing your mind. To achieve his goal, he may control you using 'crazy' techniques, causing you to feel real distress. He may tell you in his more 'pleasant' moments that he acts the way he does because he loves you so much. In reality, he's talking rubbish because the truth is, he cares for no one but himself. Nothing exists outside your abuser. He is self-centred, has a big ego and is often a practised liar. Your anguish and distress will have no impact on him and he is unlikely to feel any genuine remorse, even when the tears and apologies are flowing. Of course, he will revert to pleasant behaviour occasionally, perhaps offering to help out in the house, running you a bath or cooking you a meal, all thoughtful gestures on their own but certainly not when they are offered as an apology for violence and abuse. His remorse is really a tool to get you 'back on side', under his wing and unsure of his next move again.

Q. Does domestic violence happen during pregnancy?

A. Domestic violence often begins or escalates during pregnancy. Statistics vary but most show that between 25 per cent and 40 per cent of battered women are assaulted during pregnancy.

3

Domestic abuse and your mental health

It is now widely accepted that abuse (both in childhood and in adult life) is often the main factor in the development of depression, anxiety and other mental health disorders, and may lead to sleep disturbances, self-harm, suicide and attempted suicide, eating disorders and substance misuse. Please don't be alarmed by this as it can take years of abuse for these conditions to develop and sometimes it doesn't happen at all, but we hope that by bringing these facts to your attention, you will begin to address the immediate need to protect yourself and your children from further abuse by reaching out for help – *today*.

Below are some behaviours that will add to your distress and exaggerate any existing mental health issues. If you recognize your relationship in any of the following, please talk to your doctor or health visitor. Tell them what your partner is doing and explain how confused and paranoid it makes you feel.

Does your partner:

- say you couldn't cope without him?
- accuse you of being paranoid and mad?
- accompany you everywhere because he is your 'carer'?
- speak for you because 'you get confused, don't understand much and are not very confident'?
- accuse you of being a bad parent, and threaten to take the children away?
- tell the children that you're ill, mad, can't cope, and can't look after them properly?
- deliberately confuse you?
- hide your medication or important documents?
- pressurize you into using alcohol or drugs?
- undermine you when you ask others for help by saying things like 'don't believe her, she's mad'?

If you have been diagnosed with a mental health disorder, you will be in a particularly vulnerable position, and are likely to find it harder to report domestic violence than other women will. You may suffer from a sense of shame and guilt and be unsure about what to do.

First, please **don't blame yourself**. You are not responsible for the abuse: your abuser is. Second you are entitled to help as much as any abused person, and if you have additional support needs you should get help with these too. Your first point of contact should be your doctor, psychiatrist, health visitor or any other health professional that is assigned to looking after you.

Q. What can my doctor do to support me?

A. Lots of things. He or she can treat any injuries or depression you may be suffering from, refer you for counselling, provide practical information about domestic violence support services, and write letters to the local authority to help you and your children get temporarily or permanently rehoused. He or she will also make a note of your injuries and keep them on file should you need the records for legal purposes later on. Also, if he or she feels it is appropriate, they will help arrange emergency protection for you and your children.

Can abusers change?

One of the questions we get asked a lot is: 'Can abusers change?' The answer is yes, but it's a long process that requires undoing everything he's ever been taught. It can take years of therapy with not just counsellors but psychiatrists and other mental health professionals too. The main thing to remember is that while he may act remorsefully and play the nice guy for a while it won't last, not without prolonged therapy and treatment that involves no less than 100 per cent commitment to a non-abusive relationship. Few abusers, although some do, will commit to such a change because it is easier to go with their natural instinct to exert control over their victims.

For your abuser to change his personality, he will need to commit to a lengthy process of hard work. There are no guarantees he won't revert back to his old self and if he does change it's not going to happen overnight. It would mean unravelling everything he knows, has been taught or witnessed, breaking him down and building him back up. That's no easy task for professionals and an even harder challenge for your abuser, though absolutely crucial if he is ever to experience the joys of a healthy, non-violent relationship.

4

What is physical and sexual abuse?

You may be wondering if you or someone you know is being physically and sexually abused. Perhaps you already know you are but won't quite believe it's happening until you can identify your particular situation, either in this book or by talking to someone who has experienced the same thing. You may want to become more aware of what is happening but you are not sure how or where to look. This book will help, and confiding in as many people as possible will also give you strength and comfort. Part 6 of this book offers many useful resources, including the 24-hour UK National Domestic Violence Helpline, and support groups where you can meet others who have suffered, or are still suffering, at the hands of an abuser.

If you suspect you are being physically or sexually abused, read through the following list of behaviours and tick the ones that apply to you.

Does your partner:

❑ Grab, push, hit, punch, slap, bite, headbutt, kick, choke or pinch you?

❑ Force you to have sex when you don't want to or make you engage in sexual acts that you don't want to do?

❑ Destroy personal possessions and throw things at you?

❑ Physically hurt you, your children, pets, family members, friends or himself?

❑ Criticize your sexual performance or deliberately hurt you during sex?

How did you get on? If you answered yes to one or more of the above behaviours, you are being physically and/or sexually abused. We shall explain the differences next, but before we do, this is an appropriate time to remind you that if you sense there is any chance at all that your partner may carry out his threats of violence, whether he has beaten you before or not, it is important that you **tell someone straight away – please do it today.**

Physical and sexual abuse and how it makes you feel

Physical abuse is abuse that causes pain, injury or other physical suffering or harm. Does your partner kick, punch, hit, slap, choke, shake, scald, pull your hair, poke or pinch you, make you feel uncomfortable sexually, rape you, taunt you about your sexual performance, or do anything else that causes you pain, discomfort or injury? If a partner or family member is giving you, or your children, bruises, cuts, black eyes or broken bones, you are being physically abused. Physical abuse by a partner or family member is domestic violence.

Bruises, cuts, black eyes and broken bones are the obvious signs of physical abuse but they are not the only ones. Domestic violence doesn't always leave visible marks and scars. Having your hair pulled or an object thrown at you is violence. Being shoved down the stairs or pushed into a wall is violence. Being tripped up or having a hot drink thrown at you is also violence.

Mother of five, Alison, had her nose smashed and sight damaged by the partner she adored; Lisa was kicked 40 times in the head by her boyfriend and is now confined to a wheelchair;

Teresa's boyfriend hit her on the head with a chair leg; and Kathryn's spleen was ruptured when she was knocked unconscious by her husband and sexually assaulted in front of her two daughters. Carol's abuser made her stand in a freezing cold shower and Rita was made to get on all fours and bark like a dog while her husband kicked her in the stomach and laughed at her. Another woman, Sarah, who has now left her abuser and is happily married to someone else, was regularly locked in the garden shed all night. Her ex-husband was never physically abusive, but the psychological abuse she suffered, the verbal attacks and cat and mouse games were devastating enough.

Your partner may be sexually abusive too or he may be sexually abusive without using physical violence. Sexual abuse is when you are forced to have sex or take part in painful or degrading sexual acts – oral, anal or vaginal – that you feel uncomfortable with. If your partner criticizes your sexual performance, humiliates you in bed or deliberately hurts you during sex, you are being sexually abused. Sexual abuse includes any unwanted touching and exploitation through photography or prostitution.

Sometimes verbal and psychological abuse will be used during sex to force you to do what he wants. He may threaten to hit you, withhold housekeeping money, find another woman, leave the relationship or carry out some other punishment if you don't give in to what he wants. Does he insist on sex after physical violence to make you prove that you have forgiven and still love him? If you answer yes to that question, you are being physically and sexually abused.

When sexual abuse occurs within marriage, you may feel confused about whether or not you've been raped. The bottom line is if you say no and he goes ahead anyway it is rape, regardless of whether it's your boyfriend, husband or a stranger. When you are forced to have sex, married or not, it is rape, and when it happens within marriage it can be as cruel and soul-destroying as rape by a stranger.

MYTH: Domestic abuse victims must enjoy it or they'd leave.

FACT: Victims stay with their abusers because it is difficult for them to leave. Many women are not aware that help is available. They worry that the disruption of leaving will affect their children and fear they won't be able to cope alone. They also fear the stigma attached to being a single parent as apposed to the 'achievement' of being married.

Marriage is a contract between two people of which sex is a part. It is a contract based on mutual love and respect. Consideration towards your partner's sexual needs is a normal, healthy part of marriage, but being forced to take part in sexual acts that you don't feel comfortable with has nothing to do with love. Should this happen, he is using sex as a tool to control and humiliate you. A sexual attack will leave you feeling shocked, degraded, ashamed, guilty and terrified, not to mention in physical pain. You may have injuries that need treating and counselling will help you come to terms with the mental trauma of rape. If you need emergency treatment, call an ambulance, and make sure you report the incident to the police straight away, either by calling 999 in an emergency or by contacting your local police station. Don't let him get away with what he has done. Make him face the consequences of his actions and take responsibility for his behaviour. It's no less than he deserves.

Sexual abuse, like all forms of abuse, is always about power and control. It is a form of domestic violence and it is rarely a one-off. All types of abuse get worse with time, but physical and sexual abuse are particularly dangerous because they can lead to serious injuries and worse. Get help before the abuse escalates out of control and you reach the point where you feel you are unable to talk about what is happening. Remember it is **never too late to get help.**

> *My husband cut me off from my friends and family because he was afraid I would talk about his violence. He banned me from using the phone and locked me in the house when he went to work.*
>
> **Claire**

MYTH: Domestic violence only happens in poor communities.

FACT: Domestic violence can happen to anyone, at all levels of society, regardless of their social, economic or cultural background. Unfortunately, those on higher incomes are less likely to report it.

If you, or someone you know, are a victim of physical or sexual abuse, it is *crucial* that you talk to someone, straight away, today. Find a person you trust – a friend, neighbour, work colleague, family member or church elder – or someone you see regularly who you sense would be supportive and non-judgemental or call Refuge or Women's Aid in the UK and speak to one of the sympathetic counsellors there (see Part 6). Confiding in someone about what is happening is the first step towards ending the abuse.

Refuges are safe houses run by and for women suffering domestic violence. They are safe places where you and your children can stay, giving you time and space to think about what to do next. Refuge staff are experts in dealing with domestic abuse and will offer unconditional emotional and practical support.

Q. Do abusers and victims have low self-esteem?

A. Abusers generally don't have low self-esteem but they often pretend to as a way of getting others to believe the violence isn't their fault. Victims may have high self-esteem at the start of the relationship but the abuser uses emotional abuse over a period of time to destroy self-esteem and confidence.

Remember, the UK 24-hour freephone
National Domestic Violence Helpline
number is 0808 2000 247. (More details in
Part 6.) Call this number if you are feeling
scared, anxious or confused. There is a
sympathetic person waiting to take
your call.

5

Are you being financially abused?

Financial abuse is a common form of domestic abuse. Take a look at the following checklist, which may help you decide if you or someone you know is being financially abused. Tick any that apply.

Does someone you know:

❏ Control all your finances and force you to account for every penny you spend?
❏ Demand that you show him receipts for everything you spend?
❏ Stop you from getting a job or going to college?
❏ Deny you access to your bank accounts, credit cards, savings and loans?
❏ Limit your access to the car and other family assets?
❏ Hide bank and building society statements?
❏ Keep you short of money and basic household essentials?
❏ Insist on taking care of all household bills and domestic expenses?

If you answered yes to two or more of the above questions, it is likely that you are being financially abused. It may be that you have suspected something isn't right for some time but aren't sure how to go about proving it. It was much easier to keep giving the benefit of the doubt and avoid confrontation than face the truth and a possible angry scene. That's a normal reaction and one you shouldn't feel guilty about. None of this is your fault and, as we progress through this book, we will show you that you are not alone and there are many others in your situation, some of whom have lost their homes and life savings and many others who were fortunate to discover what was happening and get help before the situation escalated.

What is financial abuse?

Financial abuse can be anything from denying you access to funds or housekeeping money to preventing you from getting a job. The most common financial abuse occurs in a relationship where one partner is financially dependent on the other for their needs. Your partner or a loved one may be using money as a tool to manipulate and control you by making sure you are either financially dependent on him or responsible for all household expenses. If he holds you responsible for dealing with finances, he may also make it difficult for you by, for example, hiding household bills so that the responsibility of managing everything becomes an exhausting strain.

He might insist that you account for every penny spent, demanding receipts, even for small items like a loaf of bread or pint of milk. Many abusers spend money allocated to groceries on themselves. This is particularly the case when he is dependent on alcohol, gambling or drugs. He will use every trick in the book to get his hands on cash, selling household items and valuable possessions without any regret. If the children are forced to go without food because of his actions, he may feign remorse but it is unlikely his guilt will be genuine as his main concern will be for himself.

He won't hesitate to spend money on himself, even the child benefit, but will monitor every penny you spend and may demand that you hand over your salary and benefit books. In extreme cases, he may go to the lengths of forcing you to commit crimes or beg for money. Some abusers even force their partners into prostitution. As long as his needs are met and you are bowing down to his authority, he is happy.

Naturally, you may be afraid to confront your partner in case he loses his temper, physically attacks you or the children, kicks you out of the house or makes your life even more unbearable than it is already. You may be afraid that your small amount of housekeeping money will be taken away, or that he trashes your home for 'daring to complain'. We understand that you may be feeling confused and scared at what's happening. Rest assured that there are many things that you can do to improve your situation. We will discuss these, and explore many other aspects of abuse, in Part 4.

But first, let us just say that your partner refusing you access to money is unreasonable and even more so if you have children to take care of.

If he persists in making things difficult, you will need to look at other ways to financially support yourself and your children, perhaps by applying for any extra benefits that you may be entitled to. If you have already done that and he is withholding your benefit money from you, there are things you can do. Firstly, you can arrange to have his name removed from your benefit account. Then if he continues to deny you access to your money, he is committing a crime and can be reported to the relevant authorities. Talk to your health visitor – she will put you in touch with the right people and offer ongoing support.

Q. Does domestic abuse happen to the elderly?

A. Yes, usually they are abused by the people they trust the most, such as caregivers and family members. Research shows that family members commit approximately 50 per cent of financial abuse crimes against the elderly.

Financial abuse of the elderly

Abuse of the elderly is extremely common. Older people living alone can be especially vulnerable to financial and other types of abuse by family members and sometimes, but to a lesser extent, care workers. Their abuser is usually someone they know and trust.

Here are some signs of elder abuse:

- Taking less interest in things that they used to enjoy.

- Withdrawing from daily activities.

- Becoming angrier, snappy and more aggressive.

- Seeming depressed, weepy, sad, or very tired and lacking in energy.

- Fearful of being left on their own or with certain people.

- Any unusual behaviour or mannerisms.

- Seeming unusually cheerful and happy.

Of course recognizing some, or all, of the above list doesn't necessarily mean that an elderly person is being abused. There could be another reason why they are acting odd, jumpy or out of character. It is important not to jump to conclusions right away; talk to the person about how they are feeling, read through the other sections in this book, and call the Action on Elder Abuse helpline for advice on 0808 808 8141.

Do you know an older person who is displaying any of the above characteristics? Have you or someone you know become forgetful with money or lost touch with the value of money and the cost of goods? Do you know someone who has been financially organized their entire life but who has now become confused about what savings and assets they have? Do you know an elderly man or woman who has become increasingly confused, scared, weepy and nervous? Does that person sound like you? If you recognize this person, the first thing you should do is talk to your doctor so that he can rule out any undiagnosed illnesses. Then, when your health has been given the all clear, you can start to think about all the people you know and ask yourself if any have been acting oddly, differently, more controlling or abusive lately.

If you are elderly, or you know someone who lives alone and is vulnerable, keep a close eye on the people who you, or he or she, spend time with. Of course, there are many trustworthy people in the world who wouldn't dream of taking advantage of your good nature but there are also people who will – sadly even family members – so it is crucial that you stay on your guard.

The various types of abuse described in this book can apply to anyone, regardless of their age or whether they are a man or a woman. Physical, mental, emotional, verbal, psychological and financial abuse can just as easily happen to an older person as it can to a teenager, someone in a same-sex relationship, a married woman with young children, or a man in a heterosexual relationship. Abuse doesn't just happen in married relationships. It can happen between mother and daughter, father and son, aunt and niece, uncle and nephew and every other family relationship you can think of. It also happens between friends and acquaintances.

Here are some things a financial abuser may do to take advantage of an older person. Read through the list and tick any that you suspect may be happening to you.

Do you think someone you know and trust could be:

❏ Using your cash, credit cards and bankcards without your permission?

❏ Opening your post?

❏ Using your bankcard to withdraw large sums of cash from the machine without your knowledge?

❏ Promising to take care of your finances but getting you blacklisted by not paying your bills and debts and repeatedly taking out loans in your name?

❏ Forging your signature on important documents?

❏ Withholding your pension or insurance cheques?

❏ Holding your pension book 'for safekeeping' and using it to cash money?

❏ Borrowing or taking your possessions without permission?

❏ Selling your property or possessions without permission?

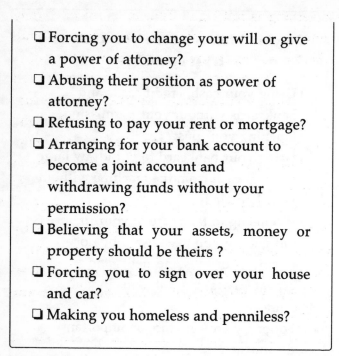

❑ Forcing you to change your will or give a power of attorney?

❑ Abusing their position as power of attorney?

❑ Refusing to pay your rent or mortgage?

❑ Arranging for your bank account to become a joint account and withdrawing funds without your permission?

❑ Believing that your assets, money or property should be theirs ?

❑ Forcing you to sign over your house and car?

❑ Making you homeless and penniless?

How many did you tick? The more you tick, the stronger you suspect someone is financially abusing you. Have you any idea who that person could be? Does anyone you know have access to your assets or bank account? Has that person been acting peculiar or out of the ordinary? Perhaps something has changed but you can't put your finger on what it is. They may call less often or avoid eye contact when they are with you. Even subtle differences can indicate that something is not right. Talk to a trusted family member or friend about your concerns and, where possible, control your finances yourself.

Ask the bank to allocate a member of staff with whom you can build a trusted relationship. Make a note of that person's direct number and keep it somewhere handy. Call that person whenever you have a financial query. Stay in control by checking everything thoroughly. File all bank and building society statements in folders and keep them somewhere easily accessible. Remember it is often less complicated, and more sensible, to have money matters dealt with by a professional person than a family member or friend.

If you suspect you are being abused in any way, whether mentally, verbally, physically, sexually or financially, call the Action on Elder Abuse helpline on 0808 808 8141. If you are in immediate danger or require emergency medical assistance call 999.

How to recognize elder financial abuse:

- A sudden change in behaviour of both the suspected victim and the abuser.

- The victim tells you someone is taking advantage of her.

- The victim develops a new, close relationship with someone who drops by her house frequently to say hello, or drives her to the bank twice a week.

- A family member starts showing a strong interest in the victim's possessions or money.

- The victim makes sudden changes to her Will.

- The victim is getting more home visits from care workers, tradesmen or 'new friends' than is necessary.

- The victim's possessions, bank and credit cards, cheque books and cash go missing.

- The victim is going without food, medicine or heat even though she has adequate funds to pay for them.

- The victim starts acting out of character, drawing large sums of cash from the machine and adding a new friend's details to her bank account.

These are most of the telltale signs that you or an elderly person is being financially abused. Perhaps a neighbour has been collecting your pension and helping you out by doing a bit of shopping for you with the cash, but not giving you any change. You then find yourself left with hardly any money for the week, or none at all. Or a family member may be asking you to sign cheques to pay your bills, and because your eyesight is failing you haven't noticed that the cheques are for large amounts payable to the person who is supposed to be helping you. Tradesmen can also financially abuse you. A plumber may carry out minor repair jobs but charge you increasingly large sums of money. Or perhaps a relative keeps asking you to lend them money or sign over rights to your house or part of their inheritance, and when you refuse he becomes verbally abusive and threatens to cut all ties with you.

Things you can do today to prevent financial abuse:

- File bank and building society statements in date order in folders and keep them somewhere they can be easily found.

- Keep up-to-date records of financial transactions and important documents in one place.

- Never sign a blank cheque allowing someone else to fill in the amount.

- Don't tell anyone your bank or credit card PIN and keep other important numbers and passwords secret.

- Don't be persuaded to put your bank account in joint names as it gives the other person easy (and legal) access to your funds.

- When in doubt, call the bank to stop cheques, freeze or close an account.

- Always consult a solicitor before setting a power of attorney or making *any* important financial decision.

- Get to know your bank manager and financial adviser. Build trusted relationships with financial staff.

- Set up direct debits to pay bills. Ask your bank for more details.

- Question any financial activity that you don't understand, large bills or invoices for services you didn't ask for.

6

How are children affected by domestic violence?

Some days you may feel you can cope with the situation at home, as long as your partner's mood swings are directed at you and not your children. When it is directed at your children, or they witness domestic abuse and violence in the one place they ought to feel safe – their home – it can add to your turmoil and confusion.

> **MYTH:** *Children are not at risk of being hurt.*
>
> **FACT:** Men who abuse their partners are likely to abuse their children too. Domestic violence is the number one indicator of child abuse.

Children often put on a brave face, but what are they really feeling? If it is early days have they been scarred? Naturally, they feel scared and vulnerable. Of course they do. They may say that they are fine to protect your feelings but really they are scared, anxious and desperate for the abuse to stop.

One of the biggest reasons women stay silent about domestic violence is because they are scared the children will be taken from them. Or sometimes it is because their partner is so lovely to the children that they are reluctant to break up the family unit. **If you are scared that your children may be taken from you, please be reassured that this only happens in extreme situations** where it becomes apparent, after careful monitoring by various professional agencies, that the children's emotional and physical well-being is in immediate danger and that adequate parental protection is not forthcoming. Authorities are reluctant to remove children from the family home unless absolutely necessary. For that reason, courts will only intervene in high-risk cases where there is clear evidence that the child's welfare is in danger.

Sometimes older children can get caught up in physical violence when they attempt to intervene. Does your partner get angrier if your child 'dares' to step in to protect you? The best thing older children can do when things turn nasty is get out of the house and call the police. Getting involved will make the situation worse, and may put your life – and theirs – in danger.

If you have older children, stress to them the importance of removing younger children from the house and dialling 999 as quickly as possible. If there is no access to a phone at home, ask them to run to a neighbour's house or the nearest phone box. The important thing is for them to get as far away from the house as possible and get help.

When children are involved there is a child protection issue. Children are vulnerable and need adult protection and guidance and if, for whatever reason, you and their father are unable to do that then specialist services will step in to protect them from immediate danger and long-term harm.

Your children don't have to be experiencing physical or psychological abuse first hand to be victims of domestic violence. If you are being abused, you may find the stress interferes with your ability to effectively parent and protect your children. They may have been told not to talk about what they have witnessed. Such a secret becomes a huge burden to a child and will cause them to feel anxious, lonely and frustrated that they are unable to protect you, their abused parent, whom they love very much.

If your children have reverted to earlier stage behaviour such as bed-wetting, thumb sucking and fear of the dark, it may be a symptom of their turmoil. Has your child withdrawn from physical contact with others and become clingier to you or another family member, perhaps acting out the abuse they are witnessing with toys or in role play with their friends? They may appear frightened and sullen and display frequent bouts of crying, screaming and whimpering. Confusion, stress, fear and shame are difficult emotions for them to deal with. What appears to be a temper tantrum can be their way of 'acting out' their conflicting emotions.

Your older children may display frequent anger outbursts and irrational fears. Sleep problems are common in children aged 6 to 11 anyway, especially nightmares, but disruptive behaviour in the home and at school can increase the frequency of night disturbances. Are they having difficulties at school, refusing to attend and finding it hard to concentrate? These are common symptoms of abuse, as are complaints of stomach aches, headaches and other pains that have no medical basis. Of course, children who are not being abused can also experience difficulties at school and make up illnesses for various reasons. Look for reasons why they may be acting the way they are and do what you can to help them feel comfortable, safe and secure.

Your teenagers, if you have them, may suffer guilt at not being able to prevent the abuse. Their reactions may be similar to yours, with anti-social and self-destructive behaviour common. Drug and alcohol abuse, self-mutilation, substance abuse and eating disorders are common among teenagers who have been victims of, or directly involved with, domestic abuse. Frequent bouts of depression, risk-taking behaviour and problems with peers and authority are also widespread.

Children and teenagers may model what they are witnessing now in their own relationships later on, equating love with pain and violence. Violence may become your child's method of dealing with stress and conflict as he grows up, but on the other hand of course, not all children who grow up in violent homes go on to become violent themselves. Some are so repelled and disgusted by what they see and experience as children that they become anti-violent and look for healthier ways of dealing with stress and conflict as adults.

However, if your son is witnessing his father beating you on a regular basis, or even now and again, it may cause him to act in a similar way in future adult intimate relationships. Your daughter may go on to tolerate abuse as an adult more than her friends who have been raised in non-violent homes. The good news is that there is less likelihood of this happening if your children benefit from intervention by the law and domestic violence programmes and, of course, it is possible it may not happen at all. Hopefully, your children will grow up to become determined not to repeat the pain and confusion they have suffered.

Try to teach your children from an early age that all violence, is a crime. How do you do that? By speaking out and getting help, dialling 999 in emergencies, talking to people about what you are experiencing and protecting your children, and yourself, by removing them from danger, by doing whatever it takes to keep them safe – by showing them that abuse will not be tolerated under any circumstances.

> *My ex-husband used to hide in the cellar and make noises. When I opened the door to listen, he stopped. I thought I was going crazy until I discovered a secret door he was using to get down there without me knowing. He later confessed to me that his dad used to lock him in the cellar when he was a child.*
>
> **Michelle**

MYTH: *Children are not aware of violence in the home.*

FACT: Studies show that most children are very aware of violence. They don't have to be direct victims of violence themselves to suffer long-term effects. Witnessing one parent attacking another can have a profound effect on their emotional well-being.

MYTH: Abusers grow up in violent homes.

FACT: Some children who experience abuse go on to be violent in future relationships but many do not because they have seen the damage it causes. People who blame violence on their childhood experiences are avoiding taking responsibility for their actions.

Q. Are abusers mentally ill?

A. Domestic abuse is a learned behaviour not a mental illness. Abusers consider violence to be an effective means to achieve power and control over their partners. Abusers are always accountable for their actions.

7

What if someone you care about is being abused?

If someone tells you that they are being abused, the most important thing you can do is believe them. A lot of research says that women and children are put off accessing services because they feel they'll be judged and not taken seriously. Encourage them to keep talking and offer practical ways to help. Praise them for being brave enough to speak up and reassure them that you will always be there for them, and will continue to be there for them regardless of what decisions they make or whether they choose to stay with their abuser or not.

Q: What should I do if I'm worried about someone?

A: If they are in immediate danger, call the emergency services. Don't be afraid to voice your concern if you suspect someone you know is a victim of domestic abuse. Remind her that she and her children are worth better treatment. Encourage them to express their feelings and suggest available resources.

One of the questions most often asked about domestic violence is: Why do people stay in abusive relationships? It's easy for someone not directly involved to say 'Just get out'. Nothing is ever that black and white in reality. There are a number of reasons why a victim may choose to stay. The most common is not wanting to be alone, closely followed by financial reasons and fear of losing her children. There is usually a hope that things will improve and love plays a massive part too. Mostly, however, it is the fear of starting over and wanting to believe things can work. It's not easy to make a decision to leave. It can take years of breaking up and getting back together before a victim realizes she deserves better.

> **MYTH:** *Domestic violence is a private matter.*
>
> **FACT:** Domestic violence has been allowed to go on behind closed doors for too long. Domestic violence is a crime, and only by speaking out will it end.

Many women also stay with violent men because they are not aware that help is available. They may not have heard of organizations like Refuge and Women's Aid, and even if they have, they may be too afraid to call or email in case their abuser is monitoring their calls or internet use. They may be locked in the house during the day with no access to a telephone or computer and if they do manage to get to a phone, they may not have the number to hand.

If you suspect someone you know is suffering domestic abuse, make her aware that there is help available. Your help will make a crucial difference to her situation, because if she feels supported and encouraged, she will feel stronger and better able to make decisions. On the other hand, feeling judged and criticized may mean she never confides in anyone again. Do what you can to make her feel supported and encouraged. Be a listening ear, believe every word she tells you, build her confidence and offer practical assistance. Help her to recognize the abuse, let her know it isn't her fault and point out that what her partner is doing is wrong but *don't* tell her to leave the relationship. Let her reach that decision by herself. After all, she might love him and think he's a good father even though he beats her.

The most important thing you can do is to **listen without judging**, respect her decisions and help her find ways to build her confidence. Her self-esteem will be low, which will affect her ability to make wise choices. Look for ways to make her feel good about herself. There are confidence-building techniques and suggestions for boosting self-esteem in Part 4, as well as a section for supporters and carers of victims, devoted to helping a loved one who you suspect is being abused.

MYTH: Women like violence.

FACT: Women do not like violence. Saying that they do is a way of justifying and blaming the victim for what is happening.

Part 2:
Emergency
Life Support

Part 1 focused on understanding what abuse is and how it affects you. It also offered detailed explanations of the different types of abuse. Hopefully, this has given you an insight into what is happening and how it makes you feel. In Part 2, we concentrate on the issue of regaining control. Here, you will find strategies for dealing with emergencies and escaping danger. We give you options on where to go from here and the organizations you can call upon for support. We help you with the immediate situation and will offer practical help and advice on dealing with the difficult times ahead. We also give you tips on how to begin taking care of yourself, physically, emotionally and psychologically.

We hope to help you figure out what keeps you in an abusive relationship. If you begin to set boundaries and enforce change, we strongly advise you to make your safety, and the well-being and safety of your children, your immediate priority. Your abuser might feel threatened by your new boundaries and react in ways you cannot predict, but please do not let that put you off taking action. There are people who want to help.

By the end of this part you will:

- Know what to do in an emergency

- Know what options are available to you

- Be prepared for an emergency

- Be aware of the various sources of support available

- Have taken steps to rebuild your confidence

- Be starting to make decisions.

8

What to do in
an emergency

If you or someone you know is in immediate danger, phone 999 or call your local police station. The number will be in the phone book. If you can't find it, get the number from directory enquiries and keep it somewhere you can get to it quickly. Please do not hesitate to call the police if you are in danger. Your first priority must be to yourself and your children. Teach your children to use 999 too, and instruct them to give the operator specific information like, 'My daddy is beating my mummy', or 'Daddy is drunk and he is hitting Mummy'. Tell them to give the operator your name and address.

You may want to consider wearing a discreet alarm or carrying a mobile phone to alert the police when you are in danger. If you have a mobile phone, keep it with you at all times and pre-programme 999 into your speed dial so that you need only hit one number. Then if you're not able to talk into the phone, but are able to press the number without your abuser knowing, the operator can hear what is happening and trace your call. You can also pre-programme other important numbers into your phone, such as a neighbour, your best friend or the number for Refuge (see page 312). If you're not able to get to a phone, look for a door or a window you can use for escape. If they are all locked, try to alert a neighbour or passer-by. Above all, make the safety of you and your children your priority.

I think my friend is being abused. She has marks on her arms and is jumpy all the time. It's so hard to know what to do. I feel guilty because I haven't stepped in, but she refuses to admit that anything is going on.

Caroline

Arrange a code word with family, friends, neighbours or your children so that they can call the police for you in an emergency. Then, if they call you at home or come to the house when things are tense, or you are being beaten, or you sense something is about to happen, and it's too risky to explain the details, you can tell them the code word and they will call emergency services.

Make sure you know every route out of the house, where you can go for help and the quickest way to get there. Memorize important phone numbers, like your neighbours' number and the number for the local police station. Memorize the numbers for Refuge and Woman's Aid (see Chapter 22). If you know someone who would be happy to offer you and your children emergency accommodation, learn his or her number by heart. Ask your neighbours to call the police any time they hear suspicious noises, or hear you screaming or crying for help. Look for the quickest route out of the house and don't worry about taking anything with you at this stage. Your priority is getting you and your children away from danger. If you are forced to leave your children behind, reassure them that you will come back for them as soon as possible. Warn them against trying to intervene in case they get hurt too. Instead, tell them where they should go to stay safe, and encourage them not to hide what is happening. Tell them that they don't need to ask anyone's permission to call 999 or run for help. At the same time, bear in mind that it isn't good for children to shoulder fear and responsibility indefinitely, and if you are having to teach your children such things, the best thing you can do for them is to get as far away from your abuser as possible. Refuges offer safe accommodation and the staff there will help you leave.

If you are at risk of violence, and he hasn't hurt you but you believe a violent episode is about to occur, do what you can to remove yourself from the situation. If that isn't possible, it may help to put some distance between you and your partner by leaving the room or refusing to get involved in an argument. Try to diffuse the tension by staying calm, as difficult and frustrating as that may be, but at the same time look for ways to escape. It is pointless arguing or disagreeing with a violent person because the only opinion they are interested in is their own. Make your safety and the well-being of your children more important than getting your point of view across. Stay calm and think of an excuse to get out of the house so that you can alert a neighbour or passer-by. If an argument does start, avoid the kitchen, garage, bathroom or any room where there is no escape route or where there is easy access to potential weapons.

When a violent episode occurs, you may need to leave your home in a hurry. If so, you can go back for your belongings later. There are people who can go with you to keep you safe. We will talk more about that in Chapter 14, and, in Part 6, we also provide you with a list of useful numbers to keep somewhere handy. For now, bear in mind that you do not have to suffer alone. You can call one of the National Domestic Violence Helplines, like Refuge or Woman's Aid, or the combined 24-hour helpline at any time of the day or night (see Part 6). They will arrange somewhere safe for you and your children to stay, and provide practical help, advice and a sympathetic ear. The Samaritans are also available at all times of the day and night, and can put you in touch with people who will help. Above all, please remember that **you are not alone** and you do not have to suffer in silence.

A summary of what to do when a violent episode occurs:

- Call 999 (in the UK) or the local police station. If that is impossible, encourage your children to get help. If you have a safety alarm or mobile phone, use it to alert someone. Call a neighbour, friend, family member or a domestic violence helpline. Tell them it's an emergency and you need help immediately.

- Look for a way to escape. If you can't escape, try to attract a neighbour or passer-by. Scream, shout, bang on walls or a window, and make as much noise as possible. Ask your neighbours to call the police any time they hear suspicious noises, or hear you screaming or crying for help.

- If you can't escape or reach a phone, get yourself and the children out of the house as soon as it is safe to do so. Take essential items only and alert the police immediately. If you or the children have been badly hurt, call 999 (in the UK) and ask for an ambulance.

Learn the following phone numbers by heart:

- Your local police station

- Your closest neighbour

- Friends and family members

- The UK freephone National Domestic Violence Helpline – 0808 2000 247

- Mankind (a telephone advice service for male victims of domestic violence and their children) – 0870 794 4124.

Before you contact any of the above, alert the emergency services by calling 999. Depending on where you live, the police will come to your aid within minutes.

MYTH: Domestic violence is a one-off event.

FACT: Domestic violence tends to increase and become more violent over time.

Q. I want to leave home temporarily – where can I go?

A. If you want to leave home temporarily, you can stay in a refuge, which is a safe house for women and children escaping domestic violence. You can contact them by ringing the UK 24-hour National Domestic Violence freephone helpline on 0808 2000 247. Another option is staying with family or friends who know about your situation and are willing to put you up. You also have a right to local authority temporary accommodation. You can arrange this by approaching your local Homeless Person's Unit for help. The number will be in the phone book or call directory enquiries.

9

Your options if you don't want to end the relationship

We have emphasized the need to make your safety, and the well-being and safety of your children, your most immediate priority, and explained what to do in an emergency. Now we begin to look at your immediate future and what you can do to help yourself and your children if you want to stay in the relationship. There are several options open to you if you don't feel quite ready to make any big decisions about leaving just yet. Part 4 covers what to do if you intend to leave the house, either permanently or temporarily.

The main thing is that we have ascertained that you are in an abusive relationship, the type of abuse you are suffering, and you know what to do in an emergency. When we consider your immediate future, we will assume that your abuser is still in the house. Part 4 explores the options open to you, and the help available, should you decide to end the relationship.

There are things you can do if you don't want to end your relationship. These include:

- Seeking counselling – either together or alone.

- Setting new personal boundaries within the relationship.

- Not suffering in silence – confiding in people about what is happening.

Seeking counselling

Whether you choose to end the relationship or not, the violence and abuse you have suffered until now will have had an effect on your well-being. The psychological effects of abuse can sometimes be more damaging than physical abuse, which isn't to say that the physical act of being brutally attacked isn't devastating enough. Being viciously kicked and beaten is not only excruciatingly painful, it is also terrifying. It may last only seconds but seem like hours, and every minute it is happening you are so scared that you are going to die and desperately want the pain to stop. You may even have wished for death, believing it would be easier than the pain of being battered.

You have suffered for long enough. It is time to take action. Let's assume for now that you have chosen to stay with your partner, and are hoping that things improve. What you want more than anything is for the violence to stop, the name-calling to end and the mental torture and mind games to become a thing of the past. You want him to be romantic, kind and loving – *all the time*.

We empathize with and understand your longing to make your relationship work. Despite what he has done, you love your partner and want things to be different. You want him to stop hurting you and the children. Of course you do. You went into the relationship with hopes for your future, you thought you'd be together forever and never dreamed that he would ever hurt you. It was such a shock when it first happened and seemed so out of character that you believed him when he said it was a one-off. Don't blame yourself for that. Why wouldn't you have believed him? His tears and cries for forgiveness seemed genuine at the time. This was the man you loved – and still do – the person you hoped to build a life with. It was easier to believe what he was saying and hope it wouldn't happen again, than suffer the heartbreak of ending the relationship and starting over.

Q. Are abusers bullies too?

A. Very much so. A bully is an expert at compulsive lying, manipulation, unpredictability, deception, denial, arrogance and attention seeking. Bullies can also be physically aggressive, emotionally and verbally abusive and play psychological mind games – all characteristics of a violent or abusive person.

We want you to consider talking to someone who right now knows nothing about you and your relationship, but will not be shocked when you tell them. They will have heard your story many times before from other women, and in some cases from men. The details of your abuse may not be exactly the same as others but there will be many similarities. There is a chance that the person you talk to will have suffered in similar ways herself and will understand what you are going through. Most importantly, she will want to help and will provide you with the emotional support you so badly need right now. She will listen without judging and will understand the many different, and conflicting, emotions that you are experiencing. She will also point you in the direction of practical help.

The person we want you to talk to is a counsellor. The UK National Domestic Violence Helpline can give you information about specialist domestic violence counselling services. The number is 0808 2000 247. If your partner refuses to go with you, please don't let that stop you from going yourself. It will help you enormously, not just in terms of having a sympathetic person listen to you and believe what you are saying, but also in terms of helping you to understand yourself, your partner and your relationship better. You may also learn more about what keeps you in an abusive relationship and will, over a period of time, be able to see a clearer way forward. Counselling helps to lift confusion, which in turn will help to rebuild your confidence. Having more confidence and self-esteem makes decision making easier. You will also come to see that the abuse is not your fault and start looking at your situation in a different way. We urge you to give it a try – for yourself, your children and your future peace of mind and happiness

It may be the case that your partner agrees to attend counselling sessions but insists he goes alone. That's fine. If there is to be any kind of permanent change in your relationship, it will only come when your partner agrees to commit to – and follow through – a lengthy process of hard work and determination. Both you and he need to commit to a non-violent relationship, and when we say that, we are not claiming that the abuse is your fault in any way because it most definitely is not. No, what we mean is that by agreeing to commit to a non-violent healthy relationship you are offering your support, and mutual support and understanding are crucial for any relationship to work.

Counselling is probably the most crucial and essential step you can take. A good counsellor will make all the difference in bringing about positive, long-lasting change. You really have nothing left to lose at this stage, having already reached rock bottom. Why not give it a try? Tell your partner that if your relationship is to stand any chance of surviving, he too must commit to long-term counselling. If he genuinely wants to change, and values your relationship enough, he will agree. If he refuses, you may have to ask yourself whether it is worth continuing with a person who has not only hurt you in the worst way possible, but also refuses to get help.

I thought that you couldn't be raped in marriage but you can. My husband forced himself on me and told me if I didn't do what he wanted he would kill me. When I struggled, he punched me hard in the face and made my nose bleed. I begged him to stop but he went ahead and had sex with me anyway.

Joanne

Setting personal boundaries within the relationship

If you are in a violent relationship, one of the most important steps you can take, as well as seeking counselling, is to start putting your own needs first. You need to learn how to set personal limits and boundaries, and how to be assertive. You may believe that taking care of yourself is selfish but your highest responsibility has to be to yourself and your children. Your partner can take care of himself. Of course, putting your own well-being and safety first will feel uncomfortable at first, and your abuser may try to make your discomfort worse by accusing you of being a bad wife or girlfriend. Please be reassured that you are nothing of the sort. Don't be put off by how uncomfortable it feels. Just keep taking care of yourself and your children, and trust that he will take care of himself, which he will, and before long it will become second nature.

Of course, there is a strong possibility that you will be too afraid to put yourself first. If this is the case, recognize that a relationship that demands you put your partner first or face the consequences is wrong and unhealthy. We recommend that you seek outside help to either escape or improve your situation. Part 6 provides many useful organizations and support groups that can help make things better for you.

When you set new boundaries by refusing to tolerate being beaten, bullied, humiliated and spoken to like a piece of dirt, you are being assertive. You are making healthy choices about how you spend your life, respecting yourself and refusing to allow another person to control your thoughts and actions. Well done! This is a positive thing to do. Setting boundaries doesn't have to mean ending your relationship; it means regaining control and taking good care of yourself and your children. It is just one of your options but a very important one that we hope you will put into practice. It will be a difficult change to make, even more so because of the nature of your abuser's personality, and his natural resistance to any kind of change.

Take small steps towards a new, assertive you. The smaller the steps, the less likely your abuser will be to notice any dramatic change. The bigger and more obvious the change, the more uneasy it will make him feel, which in turn may put you at risk of further harm. Let the new you be a gradual process with subtle changes and small steps every day and – if he is genuinely ready to commit to a non-violent relationship – he will appreciate the changes in you and support and understand your choice to be assertive.

Before we continue, it is appropriate to point out that if you set boundaries and do not enforce them, you are giving your abuser an excuse to continue with the same old behaviour. Please bear this in mind as we move forward.

MYTH: Battered women are equally to blame as the men who abuse them.

FACT: Totally wrong. Domestic violence is a choice, and the abuser is responsible for his actions at all times. Abused women make many attempts to change their own behaviour in the hope that the abuse will stop. It never does because the person that needs to address his behaviour is the abuser.

Q. Is domestic violence an anger management issue?

A. Often domestic violence has nothing to do with anger. Usually your abuser is completely in control of what he is doing but may use anger as an excuse for his actions. If he can stop to answer the phone or the door, and hit you in places where the bruises are not likely to show, he is very much in control of what he is doing.

Here are three ways in which you can begin to set personal boundaries and introduce assertiveness and change into your relationship:

1 Tell your partner exactly what behaviour you find unacceptable. For example, 'I find your belittling jokes, criticism and your controlling attitude towards me unacceptable', or 'I don't like it when you call me fat, stupid and ugly. It's not true and I won't accept it any longer', or 'Punching and kicking me is wrong and I won't tolerate it any more.'

2 Next, make it clear what you will do if he does any of those things again. For example, 'If you hit me again, I will call the police, press charges and end the relationship', or 'The next time you hurt the children, I will have you removed from the house by the police.'

3 Then tell him what you will do to enforce your new boundaries, such as, 'If you continue to threaten or harass me and the children, I will get a restraining order to keep you away from us', or, 'If you won't accept the relationship is over, I will make sure that our only means of communication is through a solicitor.'

Q. What is a restraining order?

A. A restraining order is a UK civil court order that can be issued by a judge if he or she finds probable cause to believe that the applicant has been abused or is threatened with abuse from another person. It orders the defendant to refrain from abuse and threatening behaviour, and in some cases orders that he not approach or be within a specified distance of the abused. Violation of a restraining order is a criminal offence.

We understand that communicating in this new, assertive way is not going to happen overnight. It will take a lot of practice and effort but the more you try, the easier it will become. At first, you will understandably be terrified at how he will react. The most seemingly confident people are often shaking with nerves inside, but when you are living with someone who is susceptible to flying off the handle at the slightest thing, you are likely to feel so scared that your nerves get in the way of you speaking up. As you proceed with your new assertiveness, bear in mind the unpredictability of your partner's moods, have faith that you are doing the right thing and trust your instincts. If you sense a violent episode could occur, remove yourself from the situation by leaving the room or getting out of the house, and make sure the children are safe too.

Here are some more tips for change:

- Ask directly for what you want.

- Nurture yourself and your own interests.

- Know your bottom line, that is, a limit to how many times someone can lie to you, disappoint you, cheat on you, hit you or call you insulting names before you accept that they won't change and move on.

- Be true to yourself. If a situation hurts or feels uncomfortable, acknowledge the way you feel and do what you can to make sure that you are never in that situation again.

- Value yourself – tell yourself that the only opinion that matters is your own. You can choose not to believe your abuser's accusations and insults. Keep telling yourself that you are a good wife and mother and a decent person. Your opinions are the only ones that count.

Confiding in others

So far, we have explored two powerful options when it comes to regaining control – counselling and setting personal boundaries. They may not change the dynamics of your relationship overnight, and perhaps not at all if your abuser is not willing to make an effort to change, but they will help to change *your* view of the relationship, and the way you feel about your partner. Counselling and setting personal boundaries will also give you the strength to start making wise decisions and take good care of yourself.

Now let's look at another option – confiding in others. We appreciate that talking about the abuse is probably the last thing you want to do. You will have many concerns, the main one being the imagined stigma attached to staying in a violent relationship. You may be afraid that people will judge you for choosing to stay by saying things like, 'Why don't you just get out?' or 'Why are you putting up with it?; or 'If that was me, I would be long gone by now!' Comments like these are so unhelpful and the last thing you need right now. What you want – and need – is for someone to listen unconditionally, without judging, without interfering, and without telling you what you to do. More importantly you want your feelings acknowledged and for someone to give you a big hug and tell you that they understand how you are feeling.

This book provides some answers and the kind of emotional and practical support that you need and deserve. We hope it points you in the direction of the kind of help that will enable you to make some changes in your life.

There are plenty of people who will listen without judging, people who will put their opinions aside, show care and understanding and offer support. Have a think about all the people you know. Is there someone you can talk to who will provide all of the above? Can you talk to your sister, your mum or your best friend? Perhaps, you have a close relationship with an aunt or a cousin, your brother or dad, and feel they could provide emotional support. It may be the case that the person you feel most comfortable talking to is not a family member or friend at all, but a priest, teacher, neighbour, health visitor or doctor. That's fine, simply go with your instincts, open up and let that person know what's going on. Talk to someone you trust. You may feel afraid that you won't be able to find the right words to explain how you feel. If so, tell them the facts, explain what has been going on, and allow your emotions to speak for themselves. It can be hard to stop the tears from flowing when we first reveal something we've been bottling up for so long, especially when the person we are talking to is kind and sympathetic. That's okay, let the tears flow. Hopefully, it will make you feel like a weight has been lifted from your shoulders.

Q. How do I file criminal charges against my abusive ex?

A. Call the police and give them as much information as possible, including dates and times. Tell them that you want to press charges and they will take care of the rest. If your ex pleads not guilty and the case goes to trial, you will need a solicitor. You can find one in the Yellow Pages or ask a friend or family member, or the police, to recommend one. If you are on a low income, you will get help with legal fees.

*My boyfriend is so possessive and
jealous. He doesn't have any friends and
wants to spend all his time with me. He
accuses me of having affairs with
everyone, including the postman and my
sister's boyfriend. He says he has proof
but won't tell me what it is. I know he's
lying because I haven't done anything
wrong but I don't know how to prove it.*

Jenny

10

Planning for emergencies

In Chapter 9, we covered the importance of speaking out about your situation to someone you trust – a counsellor, friend, family member, priest, neighbour or other sympathetic person – and also looked at setting personal boundaries. In this chapter, we move on to the practical aspects of planning for an emergency by exploring the need to stay vigilant and by helping you pack an 'emergency escape bag' – a bag of essential items that you will need should you have to escape from the house quickly – which will help you in the future. Chapter 11 looks at the typical cycle of abuse and how it tends to follow a three stage process.

Q. What is an emergency escape bag?

A. An emergency escape bag is a bag of essential items needed should you have to leave the house in a hurry. These include important documents for you and the children such as your driving licence, birth certificates, passports, essential medication, nappies and baby milk, change of clothes, toiletries, spare cash, toys and any sentimental items. Keep the bag somewhere safe, ideally at a friend's or family member's house, but a cupboard, under the bed or in the garage or shed is fine, as long as your abuser isn't likely to find it. Items you'll require, but use on a day-to-day basis, like your cheque book, bank cards, benefit books and address book should be kept in a handbag.

It is necessary to stress the importance of keeping your escape bag somewhere hidden but easily accessible. The ideal place would be with a friend or family member, but if that's not possible, then as close as possible to an escape route such as a door or window – but somewhere your abuser isn't likely to find it. You need to be able to grab it quickly when leaving the house. The last thing you need, or should do, when you are caught in a violent situation, is to start hunting around for your bag. Don't worry if you have to leave it behind, the most important thing is getting you and your children away from danger. You can always come back for your things later.

There's nothing to stop you putting your essentials in one place today. Find a decent size holdall, and ask a friend or family member if you can leave it at their house, and if that's not possible then put it somewhere your partner wouldn't think to look, such as a rarely used cupboard, the garage or an outside shed, and pack it with the following items:

- Passports for you and the children

- Birth certificates

- Driving licence

- Medication

- Nappies and baby milk

- Toiletries for you and the children

- Change of clothes and underwear

- A spare house key

- Other important documents, as well as a bank statement and recent utility bill (for ID purposes, these may be required for claiming benefits later, etc.)

- Anything else you want to include: practical and sentimental such as old photographs, jewellery, a few of the children's favourite toys or a teddy, your diary and address book.

Things like money, your cheque book, bank cards and benefits books can be in your handbag for daily use. Try to put everything you would need into your emergency bag, including any important documents relating to you and your children. If it's too risky to use the originals, use copies instead. If you haven't got a photocopy facility at home, you can photocopy cheaply in most newsagents and post offices. Alternatively, try your local supermarket or ask a friend if you can use their computer.

If possible, try to save a small amount of money each week. Open a separate bank account and save whatever you can afford – even if it's only a few pence per week. You can always save twos and ones in a jar and change it over at the bank once a month. You'll be surprised how quickly it will mount up, and the cash will come in handy should you need to leave in a hurry.

Of course, the most important thing is to take your children with you. If you leave them behind, things could get tricky later. Your partner may refuse to let you see them unless you return to the family home, or he may ban you from seeing them altogether. There are professional people who will help if that ever happens. We discuss this, and other legal matters, in more detail in Part 4, but for now be reassured that it is highly unlikely you would be kept apart from your children for long.

I wanted to leave but didn't know where to go. My friend said I could stay with her but I didn't want to be a burden and I wanted a proper home for my children. So, she gave me the number for the National Domestic Violence Helpline. I called them and they were so helpful. Now my children and I are living in a safe house and my ex-partner doesn't know where we are. I feel calm for the first time in years.

Jackie

Your personal safety plan

There are things you can do now to increase your own and your children's safety:

- Rehearse your escape route from the house, so that you can get away quickly.

- Memorize important phone numbers – the local police, friends, family members and neighbours.

- Keep a list of important phone numbers with you – Refuge, Women's Aid, your solicitor, the police domestic violence unit, your doctor, your social worker (if you have one), your health visitor, children's school, and the freephone 24-hour National Domestic Violence Helpline (run in partnership between Women's Aid and Refuge: 0808 2000 247).

- If you sense that a violent episode is about to occur, leave the house with your children. If that isn't possible, ask a friend or family member to take care of the children until things have calmed down.

- Hide a spare set of keys somewhere they can be found easily. Then, if he locks you in the house you may be able to escape.

- Pack your emergency escape bag. Keep it hidden but to hand, preferably at a friend's, neighbour's or family member's house, but if that isn't possible then somewhere close to an escape route.

- Teach your children to call 999 (UK) in an emergency, and what they need to say – their full name, address and phone number.

- Keep some spare change on you at all times – for phone calls, bus and taxi fares.

- Know where the nearest phone is, or if you have a mobile, keep it with you all the time.

- Arrange a safe place to go if you need to leave quickly. Tell a person you trust what is going on and ask if you can stay with them for a few nights in an emergency. Also, ask them to call the police if they hear signs of violence, shouts or screams.

- Tell everyone your code word and ask them to call the police immediately if they hear you use it.

- When there is tension, do not argue with your partner. Instead, stay calm and do not retaliate. That may not be an easy thing to do when you are being accused of all kinds of ridiculous things, or being criticized and made to feel small and humiliated, but the most important thing is that you and the children are safe.

• Keep a diary of events and any abusive phone calls, letters, emails or text messages. Keeping a record of the abuse will be useful for legal purposes later on if you end the relationship or decide to press charges.

MYTH: Domestic violence is a hidden crime.

FACT: It used to be but this is changing. Recent press attention and the UK government's pledge to address domestic violence have encouraged more victims to speak out. There are still many incidents that are not reported to the police but not as many as ten years ago. The government is committed to tackling domestic violence and bringing abusers to justice.

11

The cycle of abuse

You may or may not be aware that the abuse you are experiencing is part of a continuing three-phase cycle that can be incredibly difficult to break without outside help. Understanding the cycle of violence and how your abuser thinks will help you to see that you are not to blame for the violence you have suffered, and that your abuser is the only one responsible. It will also help you recognize when a violent episode is likely to occur so that you can plan ahead for it and protect yourself and your children.

The three phases of the cycle repeat themselves over and over, with no set pattern to their length, although each time you will probably find the abuse is more severe than the last. Over time, the cycle will probably shorten so that there are smaller gaps between incidents. Depending on how long you've been in the relationship, and how established it is, the cycle can take anything from a few hours to several years to complete, although emotional abuse will be evident in every phase, particularly the tension building and crisis phases. The cycle is shown here:

Phase 1: Tension building

Your partner:

- Picks fights

- Acts jealously and possessively

- Drinks alcohol excessively or uses drugs

- Is moody and unpredictable

- Blames you for the way he feels

- Makes you feel like you're going crazy

- Criticizes, humiliates and threatens to harm you, himself or the children.

You:

- Try to reason with your partner

- Keep quiet and try to keep the children quiet

- Try to please your partner

- Feel nervous, afraid, depressed or anxious

- Try to calm the situation

- Feel like you're walking on eggshells.

Phase 2: Crisis

Your partner:

- Verbally, physically or sexually abuses you or the children

- Has angry outbursts, punches the walls or breaks objects

- Increases control over finances

- Locks you in the house, cuts off your access to the phone or internet.

You:

- Are afraid and shocked

- Try to escape

- Call the police

- Plead with him to stop

- Pray for help

- Do whatever is necessary to protect yourself and the children

- Cry, shout or scream to attract outside attention.

Phase 3: Honeymoon

Your partner:

- Begs for forgiveness and apologizes
- May blame you for abuse
- Promises it won't happen again
- Buys you gifts and is affectionate and loving
- Stops drinking and using drugs
- Seeks counselling
- Plays down the abuse or denies it happened.

You:

- Hope that he has changed
- Forgive him
- Blame yourself
- Arrange counselling
- Let him back home or return home yourself
- Play the abuse down or deny it happened
- Hide the abuse from friends and family.

The previous lists show some examples of abusive behaviours; there are many more not listed. You may want to refer back to Part 1 of this book for further examples and insight into how the abuse makes you feel, but the main purpose of these lists is to show you the three phases – tension building, crisis and honeymoon – so that you can be better prepared for emergencies. Sometimes, the honeymoon and tension building phases will be so short that the crisis phase – or emergency phase as it is also known – seems continuous. If you are being attacked daily, you may feel like the tension building and honeymoon phases don't exist at all.

Here, again, is the number for the 24-hour **National Domestic Violence Helpline** – 0808 2000 247. Call them today for emotional and practical support.

Breaking this cycle of violence is difficult alone. This is why if you recognize yourself and your relationship in this book, it is important to seek help immediately. Living in a chaotic and stressful environment can make you doubt yourself and your ability to take care of yourself. You need outside help to enable you to see things more clearly; without it the abuse will continue. Sometimes, leaving the abusive relationship is the only way to break the cycle (see Part 4).

Why not start your road to recovery today by talking to someone? Confide in a friend or family member. Take the first step towards ending your pain by reaching out to others. There are plenty of people waiting to help and support you, and many resources available to help you understand your options. No one deserves to be abused. Do whatever it takes to protect you and your children.

MYTH: Domestic violence is just a push or a slap – it does no harm.

FACT: Domestic violence does serious harm, not just physically but psychologically. It often goes much further than a push or a slap and can result in fatal injuries. Many victims spend time in hospital and need years of counselling, help and support to recover afterwards.

Phase 1: Tension-building phase

The tension-building phase can be one of the most difficult phases to deal with. It's the phase where you feel most anxious and afraid, the one where you're walking on eggshells, desperate to please but seemingly getting everything wrong. It's the phase where you will agree to anything just to keep the peace, where you try to keep the children silent and out of his way, the phase in which you're most likely to feel scared and depressed. You try to reason with your partner and it doesn't work, nothing works, and you begin to blame yourself. It's not your fault; he's playing mind games and knows **exactly what he's doing**. He could stop but he's choosing not to. Instead, he lets the tension continue to build until one day he explodes in a fit of rage, and even though you were partly expecting it, it still comes as a shock and is still as painful and humiliating as the first time it happened.

Hopefully, this knowledge of the three phases will make you more aware of the build-up of tension so that you will sense when violence is likely to occur and take action. It will also help to have a safety plan and begin to take good care of yourself. Remember – you and the children are your essential priority. Take another step along the road to recovery by putting yourself and the children first, and be comforted that by taking these initial steps you are on your way to a happy, healthy, non-violent new life.

In Part 4, we explore in detail the road forward. In the meantime, here is a summary of the sources of support available to you.

Q. My husband locks me in the house all day and I have no access to a phone – what should I do?

A. Try to get a spare key cut and keep it hidden. If possible, get hold of a mobile phone and keep it with you at all times but don't let him know about it. If you can't afford to buy one, see if you can borrow one. Memorize escape routes and if you need to get out in an emergency, try to attract the attention of a neighbour or passer-by. Let your neighbours know what is happening so that they can call the police if they hear anything suspicious.

Phase 2: Crisis phase

The crisis phase is the peak of abusive behaviour, where things are as bad as they can get. It is during this phase that violence occurs, or a series of violent episodes or abusive incidents. Your abuser may lash out with his fists, smash up the family home, lay into you with a verbal assault, sexually abuse you, rape you or hurt your children. In most cases of domestic violence, the crisis phase is when the emergency services are likely to be called.

It is almost always followed by a period of calm, known as the honeymoon phase, where your abuser may be extremely remorseful and make promises to change and seek help. In reality, your abuser will use the honeymoon phase to regain your trust and start the cycle again.

MYTH: Battered women fall into one abusive relationship after another.

FACT: While some battered women have been in more than one abusive relationship, women who receive domestic violence help and services are less likely to enter another abusive relationship.

Phase 3: Honeymoon phase

Your abuser may come up with all sorts of common excuses during the honeymoon phase. Does he make excuses and blame you for his behaviour? Perhaps he blames alcohol or drugs or says he battered you because the house wasn't clean or his dinner wasn't ready. He may say he abuses you because he was abused as a child himself or because he's stressed at work. These are just some of the excuses he may come up with. There are many more, but most of the time he will focus on your behaviour, while at the same time wooing you back into the relationship by pleading for forgiveness and promising it won't happen again.

During the honeymoon phase, he may buy you gifts and be overly affectionate and loving, wanting to be close to you and lavishing you with praise and compliments. He may become the person you fell in love with again – thoughtful, charming, loyal and kind. He may take you out to dinner, tell you that you're beautiful, buy you flowers, or surprise you with a holiday or night away in your favourite hotel. His motive? To convince you he has changed. You may believe that this time he really will change but in reality he wants to regain control and will use whatever tactic he thinks will work.

If you have visible injuries, such as cuts and bruises, your partner may ask you to explain how you got them. As bizarre as this might sound, it is common during the honeymoon phase because he wants to distance himself from what he did wrong in order to make the relationship seem normal. He may deny anything happened at all or, if he does acknowledge the abuse, claim to have done it because he loves you so much, or because you make him angry and frustrated by your so-called infuriating behaviour. Only once he's put the blame squarely at your feet, will he apologize and promise it won't happen again. Of course, there may be occasions when he takes the blame himself. When he does, bear in mind that unless he's undergoing long-term counselling and getting help, there will always be an ulterior motive, often his determination to regain control of the relationship and keep you under his power.

As long as you're in an abusive relationship there will always be a next time. The exception, as discussed in Part 1 (Chapter 3), is when he gets professional help. Without it, the abuse is likely to continue.

Q. Who is responsible for the violence?

A. Your abuser is always responsible. During violent episodes, it may seem like he is losing control when in fact he is in total control. Your abuser can choose to be non-violent and build an honest, trusting, loving relationship with you.

Q. Are middle- and upper-class women abused?

A. Domestic violence happens in any social class. Women with money usually have better access to private resources so are able to keep the abuse hidden, while poorer women often use community services so the abuse is more likely to be exposed.

Sources of support

The police

Call the police in an emergency by dialling 999. You can also call them if you want to press charges for an earlier incident, in which case they will arrange to meet you to take a statement. Don't use the emergency 999 number for this. Instead, phone your local police station. The number will be in the *Yellow Pages* or call directory enquiries.

Refuge and Women's Aid

Both invaluable sources of support, offering practical and emotional help in times of crisis and expert advice on any matter relating to domestic violence (see Chapter 22). The National Domestic Violence Helpline is run in partnership between Women's Aid and Refuge. Call 0808 2000 247 and you will be put straight through to a warm, sympathetic person who will understand exactly what you are going through and the many conflicting emotions you are feeling.

Your best friend

Your best friend can be an invaluable source of support. She may be able to offer temporary accommodation if you need to leave home quickly. If she's a good friend, she will listen without judging and offer unconditional support regardless of what you decide to do. If nothing else, she knows you inside out and will provide comfort and encouragement when you need it the most.

Your parents

It may be that you have a wonderfully close relationship with your parents, but are reluctant to reveal what has been going on because you don't want to upset or frighten them. Perhaps they are elderly or ill, and you are afraid that telling them may cause problems for them. Only you can be the judge of that, but the majority of parents would want to know and offer support if their son or daughter was being abused. Talk to them and let them do what they can to help and protect you.

Your neighbour

A good neighbour can offer valuable support by calling the police if they suspect or hear anything suspicious. They may offer a listening ear, and be someone you can turn to in a crisis. You may want to leave a spare set of keys at their house or keep a bag of essential items there for emergency use. Any offers of babysitting should be accepted. As long as you know and trust the person you are leaving your children with, time on your own will give you valuable space to think more clearly about your situation. If your neighbour is a good friend and you trust him or her, encourage your children to know and trust them too.

Your solicitor

Your solicitor should be one of your first points of contact for any legal matters relating to your home, finances and children. Domestic violence organizations like Refuge and Woman's Aid can help you find one with a good reputation, or look in the *Yellow Pages*. You may also hear of a good solicitor through personal recommendation, through a friend or family member.

The domestic violence unit

Most police stations have a domestic violence unit with officers specializing in domestic abuse. You should automatically be referred to yours if the police are called to your home for any domestic matter. If not, call your local police station for more details. There are many things they can do to help, including fitting emergency panic buttons and supplying you with a mobile phone.

Your doctor

It is worth building a good relationship with your doctor as he or she can be an excellent source of support in times of difficulty, illness or injury. Everything you tell them is confidential and they will have records of all injuries, illnesses and conditions relating to you and your children, which will prove invaluable should you ever decide to press charges against your partner. They can also arrange emergency protection for you or your children, refer you for counselling, and provide letters of support for taking time off work and arranging local authority accommodation.

Your health visitor

Health visitors are qualified nurses with further training in health education. They work with all age groups and are there for everyone – families with young children, couples, single people, young people and the elderly. Every family has a named health visitor until their children reach school age in the UK. After that, you can talk to one by contacting your doctor's surgery. A good health visitor will listen to you, and can help, support and advise you in all sorts of situations. They will offer emotional and practical support and arrange to visit you regularly, which will make you feel less alone. Contact your doctor's surgery to find out the name of your health visitor and aim to build a good relationship with them.

Start building your confidence today

Being subjected to abuse on a daily, weekly, monthly or infrequent basis can have a detrimental effect on the way you feel and relate to others. When you feel low, you are less likely to stand up for yourself, reach out to others and make good decisions. Indecisiveness is a classic sign of having little confidence in our abilities, and putting others first without any regard for our own happiness and well-being is another sign that self-esteem has been damaged. The good news is that once you make it clear to yourself and to others that the rules have changed, people will change the way they treat you. There is more about confidence building and changing the rules in Part 4 (Chapter 18). In the meantime, here are some tips to make you feel a little better today:

- Take a relaxing bath. Add music, candles and enjoy a glass of your favourite drink – beer, tea, orange juice, or a small glass of wine.

- Avoid tension by going for a long walk. If it's cold outside, wrap up warm and walk for as long as it takes to lift your mood.

- Stop saying yes to everything. If you're a people pleaser by nature, say no occasionally and do something for yourself instead, such as either of the above two options.

- Smile! It doesn't matter if you have nothing to smile about; smiling for its own sake will help lift your mood. Do this often when you are alone (not in the middle of an argument as it could make his mood worse; it's best to stay calm and silent when tension is brewing).

- Talk about your feelings. Confide in people you trust about how you feel. Call a friend or your mum and tell her everything. Be open and honest – pour your heart out and then breathe a sigh of relief that you're no longer carrying this burden alone.

- Switch the television off and listen to some relaxing music instead. Make yourself a nice cup of tea and curl up on the sofa, even if it's just for ten minutes. Spending time alone is crucial to building healthy self-esteem.

We have reached the end of Part 2, and we hope that you are now feeling less confused and a little less scared knowing that there are things you can do to protect yourself and your children. Be assured that you do not have to suffer in silence. **There is light at the end of the tunnel**. By reading this book, you have regained a little control over your life, something that you may feel has been missing for a long time.

MYTH: Domestic violence only occurs in a small percentage of relationships.

FACT: A quarter to a third of all intimate relationships are violent. That figure applies to heterosexual and same-sex relationships.

Part 3:
Help for
Male Victims

This section focuses on male victims of domestic violence, offering practical and emotional support and insight into what is happening, and explaining the things you can do to help protect yourself. No one, man or woman, has the right to be violent or abusive towards their partner. This section shows you that you are not alone and that there are many other men who are feeling the same emotions that you are right now. We understand that you may be confused and scared about your situation, and perhaps even believe that you are to blame. We will show you that none of this is your fault, and that you have no need to feel ashamed or guilty. We will give you back some control by lifting your confusion and putting you in touch with people who can help. You can then start to think about your options, and begin to protect yourself and make vital changes.

If you are a man suffering domestic abuse you can call the MALE helpline in the UK, which is run in conjunction with the 24-hour National Domestic Violence Helpline on 0845 064 6800. Alternatively, call the UK national Mankind helpline on 0870 794 4124. Both MALE and Mankind staff are trained to support male victims of domestic violence and can refer you to a refuge if required.

The fact that you are reading this book suggests that something isn't right with your relationship, or perhaps you are seeking help for a male friend or relative who you suspect may be suffering domestic abuse. The information in this section, and most of the book, applies to you whether you are in a heterosexual or same-sex relationship, and regardless of whether your abuser is a man or a woman. Some of the practical suggestions are repeated elsewhere in other sections because much of what occurs in violent relationships follows a similar pattern regardless of whether the perpetrator and victim is male or female and regardless of their age and sexual orientation.

Whatever your situation, we can and want to help. We will explain what male domestic abuse is, what keeps men in abusive relationships, what to do in an emergency, and how you can begin supporting yourself through the difficult times ahead.

By the end of Part 3 you will:

- Understand what is happening to you

- Know what options are available to you

- Know what to do in an emergency

- Understand how to support and protect yourself

- Have more control over your life.

12

Are you in an abusive relationship?

Right now you may be thinking that you are the only man who has ever felt the way you do, but you are definitely not alone. It's hard for anyone whose partner is being violent because so many mixed feelings are involved, but it can be particularly hard for men who are on the receiving end because they don't always feel it's okay for them to admit it. Although research shows that domestic violence is most common towards women, it does happen to men too. It may be hard to admit to yourself what is happening, let alone anyone else, but right from the start we want to say that the abuse is not your fault and that there are many people who can and want to help. The following checklist is designed to help you recognize whether you are in an abusive relationship. Tick all that apply to you.

Does your partner:

❏ Physically hurt or injure you and your children?

❏ Have sudden outbursts of anger?

❏ Shout, scream and yell at you over trivial matters?

❏ Threaten to hurt you, your children or pets?

❏ Threaten to take the children away and say you'll never see them again?

❏ Act possessive and get very jealous for no reason?

❏ Make it difficult for you to see friends and family and stop you from attending family and social events?

❏ Humiliate you in front of others, call you names and poke fun at you in a hurtful way?

❏ Call you nasty names, criticize and put you down a lot?

❏ Control your finances without your permission and force you to account for every penny you spend?

❏ Kick, punch, slap, bite, hit, choke, shove, shake, grab, throw objects at you or hurt you in any other way?

❏ Destroy your possessions, smash up the home, break objects, slam doors or punch walls?

❏ Accuse you of being unfaithful?

❏ Threaten to leave you, divorce or separate?

❏ Force you to take part in sexual acts that you aren't comfortable with?

❏ Blame alcohol, drugs, stress, the children and you for their behaviour?

❏ Control how you think, act, dress, who you see and how you spend your time?

❏ Stop you from working or attending college and prevent you from doing things you enjoy?

❏ Regularly threaten suicide or threaten to kill you and the children?

❏ Tell you they can't live without you?

❏ Hide your car keys, wallet, passport or other important items?

❏ Make up lies to hurt you and tell lies about you to other people?

❏ Threaten to leave or find someone else if you don't do what they say?

Q. Is male domestic violence common?

A. The majority of domestic violence victims are women but men are abused too. According to UK Home Office statistics, one in six men are victims of domestic violence at some point in their lives.

Now that you have read through the checklist, you should be feeling less confused and more definite about whether or not you are being abused. The more behaviours you have ticked, the more likely it is that you are being abused. If you have ticked more than two, there is a high chance that you are in an abusive relationship and you should talk to someone. **You are not alone and you don't have to suffer in silence**. There are many men who are abused by their wives, girlfriends and partners every day.

The abuse may have seemed harmless at first but when it gets out of control, and it almost always does, it must be stopped before it does permanent damage to you and your children, if you have any. While we believe that everyone has the right to defend themselves, don't hit back or you may be accused of abuse yourself. There are ways you can protect yourself from domestic violence and hitting back is not one of them.

Q. Are violent women mentally ill?

A. Some can be, but it's rare. Violence and abuse is about power and control. Women who attack their partners are not normally violent elsewhere, such as with friends or work colleagues, which suggests that the abuse is deliberate and planned. No matter what the excuse, violence and abuse is never justified and being violent is always a choice.

Protect yourself by walking away – leave the room or better still get out of the house and run for help. You'll feel a lot better about yourself if you don't retaliate, and staying calm will help ease your children's anxieties and fears.

It is important that you press charges for assault if your partner attacks you. By doing so, you are sending out a clear message that you won't tolerate the abuse a minute longer. You may decide to tell her calmly that you love her but if she attacks you again you will take the children with you and leave. Be assertive and stand your ground without being physically aggressive yourself. Insist that she gets help and commits to long-term counselling and encourage her to talk to her doctor who may decide to refer her for specialist care.

Whatever you decide to do, please don't keep the abuse a secret. Let someone know what is happening, even if it's just a neighbour or the local police, so that they can look out for you. Talk to a counsellor, friends, family, colleagues, your doctor or a domestic abuse helpline. Overcome your embarrassment because you really have nothing to feel ashamed of. At the same time, remember that **your safety and that of your children is extremely important** so stay vigilant and build a safety plan. Read Part 2 for more information on safety plans and protecting yourself from further abuse.

I spoke to an old male friend in the street and afterwards my wife went crazy. She grabbed my arm and started yelling at me in front of everyone. She called me a bastard and slapped my face. When I told her to stop, she got angrier and angrier, accusing me of outrageous things, punching and kicking me. I still don't know why she lost her temper.

Thomas

Here's what to do in an emergency:

- If you sense a violent episode is about to occur, or you are being physically attacked, call 999. Tell them that you need help immediately.

- Whatever you do don't hit back or you may be seen as the abuser. Instead, remove yourself from the situation by leaving the house. If that isn't possible, go to another room but make sure it's one where there aren't objects that can be used as weapons.

- Make you and your children – if you have any – your top priority. Get the children out of the house and away from danger. Encourage them to run to a neighbour or phone for help. Tell them not to intervene or they may get hurt too.

- Call for an ambulance or your doctor if you are physically injured. Don't try to treat your injuries yourself. You have nothing to be ashamed of so please be open about what is happening and get all the help that you can.

- Don't argue with your abuser. The only opinion she is interested in is her own so reasoning with her is pointless. Make your safety your immediate priority; this is much more important than trying to get your point of view across.

- If you're not able to escape or get to a phone, try to alert a neighbour or passer-by. Make as much noise as possible. Bang on windows and walls and shout and scream if necessary – whatever it takes to get help.

No woman or man, including your partner, has the right to attack you. You have the right to protect yourself and your children and to get the help you need to make life stable and peaceful. Without resorting to violence, do what you can to protect yourself and your loved ones and make escaping danger your top priority.

We understand that most days you feel frustrated, guilty, sad and angry – all at once. You probably feel sick in the pit of your stomach, worried about leaving, and scared of coping alone. Living with an abusive partner is like emotional torture. Do you feel scared, anxious and as if you are walking on eggshells most of the time? These are common feelings for both male and female victims of domestic abuse. Being the target of a loved one's unpredictable behaviour and short temper is a terrible feeling that destroys your self-esteem, and one which can cause stress and problems in other areas of your life too, such as work and your relationships with friends and extended family.

Have you cut yourself off from friends and family because you don't want them to know about what is happening? Have you changed your behaviour or appearance to keep your partner happy? Do you stay quiet most of the time to keep the peace? Similarly, do you know a male friend or relative whose behaviour has changed recently? If you suspect or know that a family member, friend or colleague is experiencing domestic violence it may be difficult to know what to do. We discuss ways in which you can help on page 173.

MYTH: Domestic abuse doesn't happen to men.

FACT: Most people who experience domestic abuse are women but a significant number of men experience domestic abuse, as do transgender, gay and bisexual men and women.

Domestic abuse and how it makes you feel

Domestic abuse is a pattern of bullying and controlling behaviour. If you are being physically attacked then you are also a victim of domestic violence. If you are forced to alter your behaviour because you are worried about your partner's reaction, it is likely that you are being abused. Domestic abuse can take many forms – physical, verbal, psychological, sexual and financial – and it is rarely a one-off event. See Part 1 for a detailed explanation of the various types of abuse.

It is helpful to remember that all domestic violence is a crime and is unacceptable, regardless of whether the perpetrator is male or female. Everyone has the right to live without fear of violence and abuse. You may feel as though you have lost control of your life right now, but be assured that by reading this book there is light at the end of the tunnel. You can start to regain control of your life by doing one – or all – of the following:

- Call one of the support groups listed in Part 6 of this book.

- Call a domestic abuse helpline and talk to someone who can offer emotional and practical help.

- Confide in a friend, family member, colleague, neighbour, your doctor or someone else you trust.

- Speak to a counsellor.

- Press charges if your partner is physically violent to you.

- Keep a written record of every incident.

- Make you and your children your top priority.

- Be assertive and tell your partner that you will leave if she is violent or abusive again – and follow through with it.

- Remove yourself from the situation by moving in with a friend or family member or staying in a refuge.

- Work on building your confidence and self-esteem.

- Seek legal advice.

Naturally, you will be overwhelmed by fear and conflicting emotions. You will be confused about what to do because you love your partner but hate the violence and abuse. What you want more than anything is for the abuse to stop and to be a normal, happy family. You may also be struggling with feelings of guilt because your children have witnessed much of the violence and abuse. While it isn't good for a child to see one parent attacking another, there are many things you can do to protect them from witnessing further abuse (see Part 4).

Domestic violence destroys the lives of everyone involved so talk to someone about what is happening right away, today. Get the help you badly need and deserve and do everything you can to support yourself. Never hit back – walk away and always press charges. Reporting an incident to the police is one of most important ways of letting her know that you won't tolerate her abusive behaviour.

MYTH: Men who stay in abusive relationships have only themselves to blame.

FACT: Men stay for various reasons, usually because they hope that things will change, they love their partner, they are not aware that help is available, they are afraid that they will lose their children if they leave, or they are worried that no one will believe them.

The number for the MALE domestic violence helpline in the UK is 0845 064 6800. You can also call Mankind on 0870 794 4124. Both helplines can find you emergency accommodation. Alternatively, call the 24-hour National Domestic Violence Helpline on 0808 2000 247. Tell them that you're a male victim of domestic abuse and they will put you in touch with someone who can help.

What causes domestic violence towards men?

All kinds of situations can trigger violence, such as the stress of pregnancy, the death of a loved one or job loss. Frustration, alcoholism and drug abuse can also contribute to the problem. But regardless of what she may or may not say, you are not to blame in any way. If she accuses you of provoking the abuse, remember that regardless of how angry she may seem, she is always in control of her actions and can choose not to use violence and abuse and walk away. Violence is always a controlled choice.

> *MYTH: Domestic violence only happens once or twice in a relationship.*
>
> **FACT:** Violence in relationships gets worse with time. It may start with a couple of slaps and escalate in frequency and intensity. There is no set pattern to how often it occurs but it always gets worse.

Supporting male victims of abuse

If a male friend, family member or colleague tells you that his partner is abusing him, believe him. By taking his claims seriously, you will encourage him to keep talking. Many male victims of domestic abuse are afraid to speak out because they are afraid that they will be ridiculed or made to feel embarrassed, guilty or ashamed. Tell him the abuse is not his fault and that he is not alone. Domestic abuse happens to many people.

Encourage him to make his own decisions and hold back from giving advice or opinions. He wants a trusted person he can talk to who will listen without judging or offering unwanted advice. Give him plenty of time to make his own decisions and don't put him under pressure by repeatedly asking questions, especially about what he intends to do. The best support you can give is simply to be there for him, respect his need for confidentiality, listen without judging and help him to work through his options – in his own time. Give him a list of support groups and helplines that he can call, and pass on a copy of this book.

If you suspect someone you know is being abused, the following list of signs may be useful. With this person in mind, ask yourself the following questions. Tick any that apply.

❑ Has there been a change in his behaviour – does he seem distant and anxious?

❑ Has he cut contact or not contacted you much lately?

❑ Does he always worry about what his partner thinks?

❑ Does he have to check with his partner before agreeing to any social event or activity?

❑ Is his partner unreasonably possessive and jealous?

❑ Does she keep a close eye on what he is doing and who with?

❑ Is she controlling and bossy?

❑ Does she text, email or phone him several times a day?

❑ Does he have repeated unexplained bruises, marks or injuries?

❑ Has he lost control over spending his own money?

❑ Do you hear yelling, arguments and loud noises next door?

❑ Has he suddenly started taking time off work or college?

❑ Is there obvious tension in the relationship?

❑ Does his partner poke fun at or humiliate him in front of others?

The more times you answered yes to the above questions, the likelier it is that your friend or relative is being abused. We've already looked at some ways in which you can support your friend or relative, so now let's look at what you shouldn't be doing.

- Don't tell him to stay in the relationship and work things out.

- Don't offer to talk to his partner on his behalf.

- Don't tell him he should stay because of the children.

- Don't offer unwanted advice or make decisions for him.

- Don't tell him to leave.

- Don't take away your support if he doesn't do what you say.

Being supportive is about listening without offering advice. By all means suggest options – it's really important that he knows that there is help available – but recognize the difference between discussing options and telling someone what they should do. Let him make the decision about whether he stays or leaves in his own time.

Q. Are men who experience domestic violence weak and effeminate?

A. Domestic abuse is about power and control by one person over another. It does not relate to physical size. Abuse can take many forms including physical violence, but also psychological, verbal, sexual or financial abuse.

Why men stay

There are many reasons why you may choose to stay in a violent relationship. You may not know that physical assault against a man by his partner is a crime. You may feel responsible for making the relationship work or consider yourself a failure if you leave. You may feel that you have no one to turn to for support or worry about what will happen to your children if you leave. Perhaps you feel that your children need their mother, and perhaps she is lovely towards them but not to you. You may also feel ashamed or embarrassed to admit that you are being abused and reluctant to accept that the relationship is not working. Your partner may be kind and caring most of the time, and you think that you can deal with the abuse as long as it only happens now and again.

Other reasons why you may choose to stay include a fear of being alone or a fear that she will harm herself or the children if you leave. She may threaten to financially ruin or kill you if you leave, or spread lies about you. Every situation is different but male victims, regardless of the nature of their relationship, are usually terrified at the thought of leaving, and equally are terrified at the thought of staying.

Start the healing process today by talking to someone. Friends, relatives, colleagues, counsellors, domestic violence helplines, your doctor, support groups and your church are all good sources of emotional, moral and practical help. You can ask the police to take you to a refuge, or have your partner removed from the house – whatever makes you feel most comfortable and is best for everyone concerned. Remember it is better to leave home than to be seriously hurt or worse in a physical attack, so make your top priority staying safe. If protecting your children means taking them with you, then that is what you must do. The counsellors at MALE and Mankind in the UK (see Chapter 22) can help you find legal, financial and medical help and they can also find you somewhere to stay if you have nowhere to go.

Regardless of whether you decide to end the relationship or not, there is much that you can do to regain control of your life. In Part 4, we concentrate on moving forward and regaining control, and this is aimed at both male and female victims of violence and abuse. It includes a useful legal section as well as further support and advice for family members, friends and carers. We give you information on how to keep you and your children safe and discuss practical issues such as housing, finance, custody of your children and restraining orders. We also continue to offer emotional support to help you through your inner turmoil.

We hope that you will also make use of the various sources of support and help in Part 6 and read some of the real life stories in Part 5, many of which will sound familiar. Hopefully, you will come to realize that you are far from alone and that there are many other men who share your fears and anxieties. In Part 6 there is a list of useful websites as well as recommendations for further reading.

Q. Why is it so hard for men to recognize abuse?

A. There have traditionally been few services for men who experience abuse, making it hard to access support. Because they don't have much information about abuse, they may be unsure what the signs are. Men often find it difficult to talk about their experience and may cover it up because they believe it doesn't happen to their gender.

If I'm busy doing paperwork and don't have supper ready for my wife at a certain time, she flies off the handle and accuses me of neglecting her. She sulks for days, refuses to speak to me and sleeps in the spare room with the dog. I always make the first move but nothing I do or say makes her less angry. She makes me feel guilty over trivial things.

Mike

I often find myself agreeing with my girlfriend's criticisms to keep the peace. Nothing I do pleases her and lately she's started losing her temper over little things, like if I don't call her enough times a day or if I forget to buy her favourite chocolate bar. She's always telling me that I'm ugly and a rubbish boyfriend but every time I try to end the relationship she threatens to kill herself. It's easier to stay and put up with her mood swings.

Dave

Part 4:
The Way Forward

This section is about making decisions and accepting help. It is also about rebuilding your confidence and feeling good about yourself. We explore in more detail the options available to you, and offer practical and legal advice on matters such as housing, finance, custody of your children, restraining orders and future relationships. We continue to help you with the conflicting emotions that you are still feeling, and there is a special section for those of you who are supporting an abuse victim. Our aim is to equip you with enough practical and emotional support for you to make confident choices and regain control of your life. When you move on to Part 5, where we share some real life domestic abuse stories, we hope that you will be feeling much more optimistic about your future and beginning to think about the type of things that you would like to do with your life.

Remember that the UK National Domestic Violence Helpline is available day and night. Call them on 0808 2000 247 whenever you feel scared, confused or anxious about your future. If you are a man, call MALE on 0845 064 6800 or Mankind on 0870 794 4124.

In Parts 1, 2 and 3, we explained what domestic abuse is and what you should do in an emergency. We also gave some tips on what to do if you suspect or know that someone close to you is suffering domestic violence. We explored how you might be feeling and advised that you let someone know what has been happening, and accept any offers of help and support.

We hope that we have answered your initial concerns and questions so that in Part 4 we can concentrate on regaining control of your life and making important changes. We want you to feel good about yourself and the choices that you make, and to realize that you deserve the best that life has to offer. This includes being treated with respect, love and kindness by the people you choose to spend your life with.

Q. Will my confidence return?

A. There is much more chance of you getting your confidence back if you leave your abuser than if you stay. If you choose to stay, unless your abuser gets long-term help, he will continue to destroy your self-worth and sense of who you really are. Having the courage to leave in the first place will boost your self-esteem because it's not an easy thing to do. Your confidence will grow a little more every time you make and follow through a decision, change a part of your life that you're not happy with, and spend time doing things that you enjoy.

More than anything, you want the abuse to stop so that you can live a normal, happy life with your loved ones. You may question whether you love your partner after everything he's put you through but deep down you want nothing more than for your relationship to work. If there's a way that you can stop the abuse, and put it firmly behind you, you'll happily do whatever it takes. After all, nothing can be worse than what you've already suffered.

Do these thoughts sound familiar? Thousands of women, and men, around the world are thinking and feeling the same thoughts as you every day. Like you, they want their children to grow up in a stable, secure, loving household with no violence and tension. They want a strong family unit or loving partnership so much that the thought of leaving and starting again terrifies them. These are perfectly normal fears that you shouldn't be ashamed to admit. Loving relationships are the core of human life and what most people crave. You deserve love and happiness as much as anyone else.

By the end of Part 4 you will:

- Be making good decisions

- Understand your legal and practical options

- Know what signs to look for in future relationships

- Be living a happier and peaceful life

- Be starting to feel confident and good about yourself

- Know how to support someone who is being abused.

13

What can you do to stop the abuse?

The first question anyone who is being abused will ask is naturally: what can I do to stop the abuse? You don't want to end your relationship unless you really have no choice and there is absolutely no hope in changing your abuser. He doesn't seem interested in changing, so what can you do?

> *My mum met my step-dad in a pub. He gave her lots of attention and made her feel special. She brought him home to meet us after a few weeks. Even though I was young, I will never forget the moment I first met him. My first thought was how scared he made me feel. That feeling never went away.*
>
> **Jodie**

Part 2 discussed the necessity for setting personal boundaries, being assertive and confiding in people about your ordeal. We suggested counselling as an effective way to move forward. You can consider these methods as ways of confronting not just your immediate situation but also your future personal growth. There is more about personal growth and confidence building later in this section (see Chapter 18).

Now we suggest that you go one step further. Be honest to friends and family members about what is happening, and let your abuser know that you're being open about it. In other words, stand up to him in a non-confrontational way.

Abusers thrive behind closed doors. They will do anything to keep their violence a secret and present a charming front to the rest of the world. Most abusers hate the thought of people knowing what they're really like. That's why he does what he can to stop you from seeing friends and family and isolates you so that you come to depend on him totally. When he's the only person in your world, he has no fear of you telling anyone. He can abuse you as much as he wants and is confident he will get away with it because you have no one to turn to. Yet of course there *are* people you can turn to, lots of people, and you must turn to them, so that they can help to put an end to your suffering.

If you choose to stay with your abuser, it *must* be on the condition that he stops the abuse immediately and for good. Tell him that it either permanently stops today or you will leave and take the children with you. A word of caution here – when you give an ultimatum you *must* follow it through or he may never take you seriously again. No matter how many ultimatums or threats to leave you've made in the past and broken, decide right now that whatever ultimatums or threats you make in the future you will follow them through.

Start reclaiming some of your power by talking to people. Grab any offer of emotional and practical help that comes your way and put feelings of guilt, shame and regret to one side, as difficult as that may be. Your feelings are real and very raw, but it's only by pushing through them and seeking help that real change can occur. Be brave and reach out today by calling the National Domestic Violence Helpline on 0808 2000 247.

MYTH: Victims exaggerate the violence that happens to them. It is never as bad as it sounds.

FACT: Untrue! Victims usually cover up domestic violence because they feel ashamed, guilty and embarrassed and blame themselves.

A word of warning

Standing up to a bully is one of the best ways of stopping them in their tracks, but it can also make them extremely angry – often even angrier than before. Consequently, it's crucial that you stay vigilant and tread carefully in order not to make your situation even more unbearable. Letting your partner know that you won't stand for it anymore is a useful tactic if the abuse is verbal, financial or psychological, but if your partner has already been physically violent to you on one or more occasion, or you instinctively sense that standing your ground will tip him over the edge into violence, it is crucial that you take some safety precautions before proceeding.

First, tell your local police about the situation and ask them to keep a close eye on you. Most police stations have domestic violence units who will provide you with a safety device that you can use in the event of an emergency. These include a panic alarm that you can carry around with you – the preferred option – or fit in discreet places around the house. The alarm is directly linked to your police station so that when you activate it they can rush to your aid. Carrying one around with you, whether hidden up your sleeve, in your shoe, on your wrist, or in your purse, will instantly make you feel more comforted and confident.

Second, ask a neighbour to call the police straight away if they hear suspicious noises or don't see you around for a few days. Pre-programme your neighbour's number into your mobile phone, if you have one, along with other emergency numbers, so that you need only press one button in emergencies. If your abuser checks your phone, memorize the numbers instead. Think of a special code that will let neighbours, friends and relatives know that you need assistance. For example, if they phone and you say the word 'Sunday' or 'milk' – or any other random word that has been agreed between you – or if you call and let the phone ring once before hanging up, they will know it's a cry for help and call the police.

Other safety measures include:

- Removing potential weapons from your house such as sharp knives, glass bottles and tools. Of course, it isn't practical to remove them all as most everyday objects have the potential to be used as weapons, but clearing your home of some will help you to feel more secure.

- Buying an extremely loud whistle or keyring alarm and carrying it around with you. Go for the type that are designed to deter rapists because they are specifically made not only to alert attention by being painfully noisy but also to stop your abuser in his tracks – long enough for you to escape from the house. You can buy one over the internet quickly and easily. The Suzy Lamplugh Trust in the UK sells personal shriek alarms that claim to be the most effective personal alarms on the market.

- If you don't have a mobile or home phone, making a mental note of where your nearest phone is, whether it's a phone box or a neighbour's phone. Be ready to run to it or get your children to if you need help.

Remember – stay vigilant, prioritize your safety and the safety of your children above everything and speak out with confidence. The more confident you act, even when you are shaking like jelly inside, the more confident you will feel. If you plan to let your abuser know that you are reaching out to others, take safety precautions first, and never apologize for speaking out or justify your actions in any way. You have every right to seek help. If he doesn't like it, remember that he shouldn't be abusing you in the first place.

> *MYTH: It is easier for gay and lesbian victims of domestic violence to leave than heterosexual victims.*
>
> **FACT:** Gay and lesbian couples find it just as difficult to leave abusive relationships as heterosexual couples. Like any couple where domestic abuse is involved, they may return several times and experience many violent attacks before ending the relationship for good.

14

Your options if you decide to leave

Most people, when you tell them about your situation, will encourage you to get out of your relationship. This is because they don't really understand what you are going through. What many people don't realize is that deciding to leave is a tough choice to make. Sixty per cent of women leave because they fear that if they don't they or their children will be killed. This decision is mostly based on terror of what may come next, not because you've fallen out of love with your partner or want to be single again, although that can sometimes be the case.

When you leave, you may have to give up everything for the time being, such as your house, financial security and most of your possessions, but don't let that stop you. Material possessions can be built up again, and when you feel strong enough you can fight for what is rightfully yours with the help of a good lawyer. Your life and mental well-being are the most important things so please stay strong. If you've been repeatedly told that you're incompetent, stupid and an idiot, you may have difficulty believing that you can survive on your own, and you will understandably be petrified. Your partner has dictated your every move and controlled your thoughts for so long that it's only natural for you to question whether you can survive without him. However, most women – and men – who leave abusive relationships, some of whom spent over 30 years living in fear, say that there is life after abuse. Not only that, they say that it's better than they ever expected it to be. Trust us when we say that **leaving can never be as bad as staying**.

When I bought our daughter a new pair of school shoes my husband didn't speak to me for five days. When I explained that her old shoes were falling apart and that she was being bullied at school because of it, he accused me of being soft and said I spoiled her. He also accused me of being a spendthrift. He demanded a receipt for the shoes and the 51p change, and when I said I didn't have it he exploded with rage and threw her new shoes in the bin.

Mary

In the early months when you first leave, you may find that you can barely function. Everything will be overwhelming. Dealing with everyday, normal activities may take a lot of effort. When you are alone, you may spend most of your time crying and you may wonder whether leaving was in fact the right thing to do. You will naturally miss your house and you may miss the 'family unit' of which you were once part. These feelings can be especially overwhelming when you've had to leave everything behind and start again from scratch. Hopefully, you will have managed to take your children with you, but if you are forced to leave them behind and are unable to return for them later, there are ways the law can help. Domestic abuse organizations like Refuge and Woman's Aid will put you in touch with a good solicitor who will fight on your behalf.

You probably think that the woman you once were has gone forever, but she's still there, and you will find her again. You may be exhausted by years of pain, frustration, resentment and unresolved hurt, but every day that you are away from your abuser is another day in the healing process. Gradually you will become stronger, and with determination you will fight your way back.

When you leave, your abuser will probably continue to try to control your life. Things may get worse before they get better so it's vital that you take special care when leaving. Set up a good support system to help you through the difficult times ahead.

The law is on your side, and Refuge and Women's Aid – and for men the MALE and Mankind organizations – have lots of experience dealing with domestic abuse. They will offer practical advice and help on staying safe, put you in touch with people who will protect you, and arrange safe accommodation if required. Your abuser doesn't have to know where you are if you don't want him to. There is more detailed advice about safety precautions on page 218. But for now be reassured that **there is life after abuse.**

What housing options are available to you?

Staying at home

Your housing options will depend on your personal circumstances. If you decide to end your relationship, you will probably want to stay at home and get your abuser out of the house, and this can be arranged, particularly when there are children involved. Of course, it won't be easy as it's unlikely that he will leave of his own free will, and he may keep returning until an injunction order is in place. An injunction is a legal document drawn up by a court judge that stops him being violent and approaching you, your children and your home. We discuss injunctions in more detail on page 230 and offer safety tips should you choose to stay at home on pages 218–21. For the moment, bear in mind that you don't have to leave home and that there are people who can help make life bearable for you, and prioritize your safety above everything else, when you ask him to leave.

The people you need to talk to are:

- The police

- A solicitor

- Your landlord or mortgage provider

- Friends and family

- Your neighbours

- A counsellor

- The domestic abuse helpline on 0808 2000 247.

If your abuser's name is on the mortgage or rent book, there will be practical and financial matters to deal with. The best person or organization to approach depends on your housing situation. If you and your partner own the house, you will need to explain your situation to a solicitor. He or she will offer advice from a legal point of view and help you to make arrangements for the house to be sold or for it to be transferred into your name only. On the other hand, if your house is rented from the local council or you are privately renting in joint names, you have two options:

1 Speak to the council about getting his name taken off the rent book. You will need to explain that yours is a domestic violence situation and show them any legal paperwork like a restraining order or letter from your doctor. It may help to ask a solicitor to speak on your behalf. You can also seek advice from the National Domestic Violence Helpline 24 hours a day on 0808 2000 247. If your abuser continues to make life really difficult, it might be worth speaking to the council about a transfer to another house or area.

2 Talk to your private landlord about amending the tenancy agreement. Ask for it to be changed to your name only. If this isn't possible, you may want to look for alternative private accommodation when your current tenancy ends. Again, you can call the National Domestic Violence Helpline on 0808 2000 247 to talk about this and other practical matters.

The main advantage to staying at home is that you will not need to disrupt your life, or your children's lives, by moving from your familiar surroundings and possibly from a close support network of friends and family. You need to weigh this up against the risks involved and against whether there is a high chance of the violence getting worse if your abuser is made to leave the house. You can get an injunction within 24 hours to stop your ex-partner coming near the house or approaching you and the children. However, if he is likely to keep breaking court orders, and many abusers do, it might be less hassle in the long term to find somewhere else to live and not give him your new address or phone number.

You also need to consider your finances because it may be too expensive to run the house by yourself. Seek advice on any benefits you may be entitled to and get expert help with your finances by calling your local Citizen's Advice Bureau; the number will be in the phone book. Alternatively, call the National Domestic Violence Helpline or one of the many other helplines dedicated to helping survivors of abuse (see Part 6).

Should you leave your accommodation?

Only you can decide, but if you're at risk of violence you may need to leave your accommodation temporarily for your own protection, at least until you can sort out your situation. If this is what you decide to do, try to arrange alternative accommodation before you leave home. The ideal option is to stay with friends or relatives, but this is usually only a temporary measure. It gives you time and space to work out your options but you will eventually want to arrange something more permanent. You will need to consider the risk of further violence if your partner knows your whereabouts, and the risk of violence towards friends and family members who may not know how, or be properly equipped, to protect you from danger.

With this in mind, if you need to leave home quickly, your safest option is to contact a refuge. You can do this by calling the domestic abuse helpline on 0800 917 1414. A refuge can offer support not usually available in other temporary accommodation such as bed and breakfasts, hostels, and hotels. The refuge staff have specialist knowledge of domestic abuse so they can offer expert support and advice on practical and legal matters like finance, claiming benefits, getting injunctions, work and childcare, permanent housing and staying safe. You can take your children with you, and your abuser will not know where you are because the address and contact details of all refuges are kept secret.

Refuges

Refuges look like, and usually are, ordinary houses or purpose-built accommodation specially equipped for women and children escaping violence and abuse. The staff are mainly women who are often survivors of domestic abuse, and you will share the house with other women and children who have experienced domestic violence, threats or abuse. Sharing similar

Q. What's it like in a refuge?

A. Refuges are like normal houses but the addresses are kept secret. You usually get a room to share with your children, and share the rest of the house such as the living room, bathroom and kitchen with other women and children. No male visitors are allowed and staff will offer advice and support you with practical and emotional worries.

experiences means you can help and support each other and you may find yourself making new friends in the process.

In most refuges you will get a room of your own for you and your children, and share a living room, bathroom and kitchen with other residents. You will be asked to keep the address secret to protect you and other residents staying there. Refuges don't allow male visitors under any circumstances. They will know what to do, and be able to protect you, if your abuser finds out where you are staying.

You can stay for as long as you want, from a few days to several months, and if you decide to go back to your ex-partner, there is nothing to stop you returning to the refuge if things turn nasty again. Staff there will never judge you or question your decisions because they understand how difficult leaving an abusive relationship can be. They know that it often takes lots of going backwards and forwards before making the break for good, and they will continue to offer practical and emotional support as you work out your situation.

The quickest way to get a place in a refuge is by calling the domestic violence helpline on 0808 2000 247. Make sure you are in a safe place when you contact them as they might need to call you back. If it's an emergency, they will make arrangements for the police to collect you and take you there or you can go by taxi or car if you have one. Another option is to call the police yourself and tell them you need to get to a refuge quickly. The police will protect you if your abuser returns home suddenly while you are leaving.

If you would prefer not to stay in a refuge, your other housing options include:

- Renting from a private landlord

- Applying as homeless to a local council

- Buying a property.

Men suffering abuse should contact MALE on 0845 064 6800, Mankind on 0870 794 4124 or the domestic abuse helpline on 0808 2000 247. All three will help you find somewhere safe to stay.

Renting from a private landlord

This is usually the most expensive option, and the quality of private housing can vary so it pays to shop around. Look in your local newspaper for private adverts or ring around some letting agencies. You will find the numbers in the *Yellow Pages* or on the internet. Most private landlords ask for a deposit equal to one month's rent plus a full month's rent in advance when you sign a tenancy agreement. If you are claiming housing benefit, you will need to find a landlord who will accept it as not all of them do. The same applies to pets. You will also need to consider whether you require furnished accommodation or unfurnished. This will depend on what you are able to take with you when you leave your abuser.

Applying as homeless to the local council

This is easy enough to do when you know how. All it takes is a quick phone call or a visit to your local council offices. Staff there will give you all the necessary forms and you will be able to make an appointment to discuss your situation with a housing officer. If you need help filling out forms, contact your local Citizen's Advice Bureau or if you are staying at a refuge, ask one of the staff there for assistance. Alternatively, you could ask a friend or relative for help or call the National Domestic Violence Helpline on 0808 2000 247 and ask them to put you in touch with someone who can help.

Once you've registered as homeless, how quickly you are allocated housing depends on your personal circumstances. If you are staying with friends or family, the housing executive will probably consider you homeless. The same applies if you're staying in a bed and breakfast, hostel or refuge. You will be classed as top priority if you have children, and housing officers will also take into account any threats and intimidation from your ex-partner. You will usually have to wait longer for accommodation if the housing executive decides that you are not homeless and you will be put on a waiting list for permanent accommodation.

Buying a property

If money is not an issue, you may consider buying a property in your name only. How quickly you get to move depends on how quickly you find a suitable property, whether you need to sell another property first, and if there are complications with the selling process. The owners of the house you want to buy from may also need to find suitable alternative accommodation, but as a general guide house purchases can take up to four months to complete, or longer in extreme cases. The average time to buy is about 12 weeks, but that is not practical if you need to leave home quickly. An alternative is to stay in a refuge and make arrangements to purchase a property from there.

What should you take with you?

Part 2 talked about how important it is to pack an emergency escape bag, and gave you some ideas of what to put in it. We mentioned important documents, like passports, birth certificates and bank books, and suggested that you include a few of the children's favourite toys, a change of clothes and toiletries. We also suggested that you take a few personal items, particularly if something has strong sentimental value, and some family photographs. Nappies, baby milk, medication, your cheque book and house keys are also important. Depending on where you are going, you may need to leave larger items like furniture until later. Basic essentials are provided in refuges and in most bed and breakfasts.

Take enough clothes to last a few days. You can return for more when it is safe to do so, and you can collect anything else you want at the same time. If it isn't safe to return home, you can do so under police escort. Don't worry too much about taking possessions with you at this stage. Providing your abuser doesn't destroy the rest of your belongings, and some men do just that as a way of punishing their victim for leaving, you can get the rest of your things when the situation has calmed down. You and the children are most important. Material possessions mean nothing compared to life, health and well-being.

Q. What about my pets?

A. Many local animal charities will accommodate pets temporarily in cases of domestic violence and abuse. Or you might feel more comfortable if your pet is staying with a friend or relative. A useful organization is the Ease Pet Fostering Service for animals of women and children fleeing domestic violence. Call them on 07789 697398.

Safety and protection

One of the most important things to consider when leaving an abusive relationship is your safety. Regardless of whether you stay in your home or move to different accommodation, you will need to take basic precautions to protect yourself and your children. You need to constantly think one step ahead, at least until things have calmed down.

Leaving a violent relationship is not easy but it's a far better option than staying, and there are many people who can help keep you safe, including the police, refuge staff, your solicitor and domestic violence experts. Closer to home, your friends, family members and neighbours can also look out for you, phone you regularly and be on call should you need their help.

Here are some further tips on staying safe:

- Programme emergency numbers into your mobile phone.

- Buy a personal shriek alarm and carry it with you – somewhere you can activate it quickly like around your wrist or neck. If it's handheld, wear clothes with pockets and keep it there.

- If you're staying at home or moving to a place where it's just you and the children, consider installing basic security system. If your abuser still has a key to your house, have the locks changed. You will find the number for a locksmith in the *Yellow Pages* or on the internet if you have access to it.

- You can change your phone number if you receive abuse by phone. Call your telephone service provider; most will do it for free if you're getting abusive calls. If he keeps calling your mobile, consider buying a new SIM card, which will give you a new number. You can buy them from mobile phone shops and most supermarkets.

- If you have children at nursery or school, tell their teachers and nursery staff the names of the people allowed to collect them. Introduce them to those people so they can put a name to the face. Ask them to call you immediately if there are any problems, or if the children are snatched. This shouldn't be the case if the staff know your situation and the people who are allowed to collect them. Most nurseries and schools have security systems in place now so visitors have to buzz and give their name. Your abuser could pretend to be somebody else so make sure you've introduced staff to the person picking your children up.

• Keep friends, family members and refuge staff informed of your movements. If you're going out, tell them where you are going and who with, what time you're likely to be back, and how they can contact you. It sounds obvious, but never accept a lift from a stranger or someone directly involved with your abuser because they may be helping him by taking you to him. Stay in busy places and run to a shop or the nearest house for help if your abuser shows up. Don't get drawn into an argument – walk away or better still don't start talking to him in the first place. If he's trying to talk to you about access to the children, tell him you will talk when someone else is present. We discuss the issue of children in more detail in Chapter 16.

• Change your routine – use different shops, travel routes and services to the ones you used when you were with your abuser. This lessens the likelihood of him finding and following you.

- There may come a time, especially if you have children, when you need to talk to your abuser. Think of safe ways to do this, such as making sure someone else is in the room, and talking in the presence of a counsellor, mediator, solicitor, mutual friend or relatives. Press 141 to withhold your phone number when using a landline (in the UK), and withhold your phone number when calling from a mobile by activating the related feature on your phone. You can also arrange for the police to listen in to the call.

MYTH: Refuges in the UK only accept British women and their children.

FACT: Refuges accept all women who've experienced physical, emotional or sexual domestic violence regardless of race. There are also some refuges specifically for Asian, African-Caribbean, Jewish and Irish women.

15

How the law can help

The law can help in many ways. If you are violently attacked, you can have your abuser arrested for assault, rape or attempted murder. If he holds you against your will, you can have him arrested for false imprisonment, and if he destroys your possessions, your car or property, you can press charges for criminal damage. He can also be arrested for harassment if you have ended the relationship but he won't leave you alone.

Not every form of domestic violence is illegal – emotional and psychological abuse aren't but some aspects of financial abuse are. For example, you can press charges for fraud if someone is interfering with your bank account, stealing your cash or forging your signature on important documents. If someone has stolen money from you, a solicitor will represent you in court and, if there is enough evidence and the person is convicted, he may be ordered to repay you the cash, plus interest and expenses. You may also be awarded something to compensate for the stress that you have suffered. You may feel that no amount of money can make up for the terrible ordeal that you have suffered, but it will go some way towards easing your financial situation, which is one less thing to worry about. What you can and can't press charges for depends on your particular circumstances, so explain your situation to the police or your solicitor and they will advise you accordingly.

Of course, you may be afraid to tell the police in case it makes your abuser angrier and the violence worse. Alternatively, you may want your abuser arrested and kept in a cell overnight but not taken to court. It could be that you just want to shock him enough to realize the mistake he has made, or to get him to show some genuine remorse. Whatever your reasons, you are not alone in feeling that way. There are many women, and men, struggling with conflicting feelings of love and hate, anger, guilt and indecisiveness. You may be afraid that if you call the police and he is arrested and held in a cell overnight he won't want to come home if he is released, or he will carry out his threats to commit suicide or disappear out of your life for good. Despite everything, you still love him and want him in your life. You don't want to do anything that may result in him harming himself or leaving you alone with the children.

It is okay to feel that way and nobody should judge you for it. Only people who have lived with domestic violence can truly understand the feelings involved. However, even though there are many harrowing stories in the media about men, and women, killing themselves or their children as a form of punishment for something they have supposedly done, it is still rare. It is more common for an abuser to stick around and taunt his victims with threats to kill than actually to go through with it. Moreover, it is unlikely he will leave you if you press charges because ending the relationship means letting go of the power and control he has over you, and that's something he fears losing the most. His immediate thoughts are more likely to be about losing you and finding a way to keep you on side and convince you he can change. So go ahead and press charges and show him that you won't tolerate his abuse for a minute longer.

Here's what's likely to happen when he's arrested:

- He'll be taken to a police station, charged with whatever crime he has committed, and then either released on bail or kept in custody until the court case.

- If he's released on bail, there will probably be certain conditions attached, such as not being allowed to approach you and your children and being ordered to stay elsewhere. If he comes near you or contacts you by phone, or sends messages via someone else, he will be taken back into custody and kept there until the court hearing.

- If he pleads guilty, the process is a lot quicker. He will be sentenced immediately, or within a few days. You won't have to go to court but you will probably be asked to provide the court with a victim impact statement, describing the effect the abuse has had on you. The court will take your statement into account when sentencing.

- If he pleads not guilty, the case will go to trial and you may be called to give evidence. There are people who can help if this happens. Organizations like Victim Support (see page 313) will answer any questions you have and support you through the court process.

- If your abuser won't leave you alone, is calling you frequently, threatening you by text message or email or following you and turning up at your house uninvited, you can press charges for harassment. If he's convicted, he can be sentenced to up to five years in prison under the UK Protection from Harassment Act.

If you're being stalked or harassed by your ex-partner, or have left home and are worried that he will find you, consider taking out an injunction to give you and your children better protection. It will also give you more peace of mind knowing that he is banned by law from coming near you, turning up at your door, phoning or sending email or text messages. He may also be banned from contacting you indirectly through someone else. The main purpose of an injunction is to help keep you safe, and if he breaks the law by contacting you, he will be arrested and most likely charged and kept in custody.

To apply for an injunction, you have to go to court. The only people in the courtroom will be professional people directly involved with the case. Your address can be kept secret if you request it, and if you're struggling financially you can get help with legal costs. If you can afford it, your solicitor should be your first point of contact. Otherwise, call the Rights of Women for free and confidential advice on 020 7251 6577. Male abuse victims should call MALE for advice on 0845 064 6800 or Mankind on 0870 794 4124.

My husband told me that if I divorced him he would make sure I didn't get a penny from the courts and he would fight me for custody of the children by telling them that I was a drug addict, an alcoholic and unfit mother. None of it was true. Still, I was terrified that I would lose my children but couldn't live with his violence another day so I left with the kids while he was at work. We stayed in a refuge for nearly three months before the council put us up in a flat. My husband eventually found out where we were and tried to take the children away from me, but thankfully the courts ruled in my favour. I'm now married again to a lovely man and have another child. We haven't seen or heard from my ex for more than three years. The last I heard he was living with a woman and doing the same to her as he did to me.

Deana

The law can also help you to keep your children in the event of separation or divorce. A common control tactic used by many abusers is to threaten to kidnap or get custody of the children. They use custody and visitation arrangements as a way to re-establish control and make you feel intimidated. He may also use the legal system to punish you for leaving.

It is unlikely that any court would give your ex-partner custody of the children if he is violent and abusive. To help strengthen your case, keep a record of every violent incident, threats to hurt you and the children, harassment and intimidation. Keep a detailed diary of everything that happens and make a note of the times and dates, and get a friend or relative to take photographs of any injuries inflicted on you or the children. Every piece of evidence, no matter how small or insignificant it seems at the time, will help if you have to go to court. Remember, there are plenty of people who will support you through the whole process, so if he threatens to take the children away seek legal help immediately.

Many people wrongly believe that to stop the abuse all a victim needs to do is leave, but that is not the case. Most victims not only have to fight a legal battle for what is rightfully theirs, but also endure continued abuse, taunts, intimidation and harassment. If this is something you suspect may happen, get as much advice and support as you can. The fact that leaving can be dangerous does not mean that you should stay. Continuing to live with him may be more dangerous than leaving because violence gets worse with time. You should get as much support as possible to safeguard you and your children if you leave.

Violence, intimidation and harassment are illegal and punishable by long prison sentences, so bear that in mind as you move forward. Remember, too, that the bigger your support network, the more secure you will feel, and with the right help you can stop the abuse for good. Stay strong and keep fighting for the happiness and peaceful stability that you and your children deserve.

MYTH: The law doesn't protect victims of domestic violence.

FACT: Yes it does. Domestic violence is a serious crime and punishable by law.

Your finances

One of your big worries might be finance. In fact it could be one of the main reasons why you have been afraid to leave your partner until now. If you have been used to a comfortable lifestyle and he has threatened to leave you penniless if you walk out, your concerns are natural and under-standable. Don't feel guilty about wanting your home comforts – being surrounded by nice things is something that most people strive for. However, ask yourself: is a comfortable lifestyle really worth putting your life at risk for? Is it worth suffering unbearable abuse and violence for money in the bank and material possessions? Okay, you may struggle to make ends meet for a while, but things will improve again. Besides, there are people who can help you fight for what is rightfully yours so leaving doesn't have to mean losing everything, regardless of what he wants you to believe.

Let's consider your financial rights for a moment: What you're entitled to depends on your personal circumstances and whether you are married or co-habiting. If you're married, you will probably be entitled to claim:

- A lump sum cash settlement

- Regular maintenance payments for you and the children

- A share of your ex-husband's pension

- A share of the profits in your home

- Some of the assets you have built up together such as cars, jewellery etc.

If you're not married, but have been living together for some time you may still be able to claim something, particularly maintenance for your children and some of the assets you have built up together. You will also be entitled to a share of the profits in your home if it's in joint names. We suggest you **seek legal advice** to clarify exactly what you are entitled to as soon as possible after leaving.

One thing you will need to consider is how you're going to support yourself and your children while you wait for your financial settlement to come through. If you're not entitled to anything, or your ex-partner doesn't have any money or assets to share, you will need to find other ways to support yourself financially.

In the UK, if you work 16 or more hours per week you may be entitled to child or working tax credit, which is a regular amount of cash from the government to top up your salary or help with childcare fees. If you're on a low income you may also be entitled to housing benefit and you will continue to receive child benefit if you have children, regardless of whether you work or not. Call Rights of Women on 020 7251 6577 or your local Citizens Advice Bureau for free advice, and once you have secured your share of the finances, remember to make arrangements to have your name removed from all joint finances, credit cards and bank accounts. The Citizens Advice Bureaux are the best people to talk to for help with that.

16

Your children

If you have children, and you need to escape from the family home quickly, do what you can to take them with you. It is never a good idea to leave them behind because he may make it difficult for you to get them back or see them. However, if you're forced to leave them, your first point of contact should be a solicitor, closely followed by a Woman's Aid or Refuge counsellor to help and support you through the process of getting them back (see Part 6). They will let you know where you stand legally and give advice on what to do. Your solicitor will speak to court officials on your behalf and will know how the law works in your particular circumstances. Hopefully, your children will not be parted from you for long. With the right help and support, you will get them back and can then concentrate on your options, and support yourself and your children through the times ahead.

Q. Can I take my children to a refuge?

A. You can stay in a refuge with your children for as long as you want. Refuges are safe houses for women and children escaping domestic violence. However, some refuges don't take boys over the age of 12 so tell them your children's ages when you call and if you're not able to take all of your children with you, they will let you know what your options are and put you in touch with people who can help. They will make the safety of you and all of your children a priority.

Depending on the ages of your children, you may want to arrange counselling to help them with the healing process. They may say that they are fine and don't want to talk about it, preferring to block out what has happened and put it behind them. Of course, you should take their wishes into account, particularly if they are teenagers, but if they have witnessed or directly suffered much of the abuse, it will be in their best interests to work through their emotions with a professional counsellor. Bottling things up is not healthy and may cause long-term problems. Encourage them to be open about their feelings, and seek advice on what professional help is available.

Q. How can I rebuild my children's confidence?

A. Pay attention to the things they say and offer lots of praise. Listen when they speak and spend quality time together. Sign them up for new activities and encourage their interests. Have lots of heart-to-heart chats. Question them about their day, find out what's going on with their friends, and support and encourage them at every stage of their growth. Tell them you love them daily and offer plenty of hugs. Spend time helping with homework and reading books together, and always eat as a family at the dinner table. Do lots of other things together as a family too.

Other ways in which you can help your children include:

- Talking to them and encouraging them to share their feelings. Ask them how the abuse made them feel and reassure them that you are doing everything you can to keep them safe.

- Give plenty of hugs and reassurance that you love them.

- Be patient. Children react to abuse in different ways and often start misbehaving as a way of dealing with their inner turmoil. This is not uncommon and usually settles down fairly quickly with good support. Stay calm and walk out of the room if they are having a tantrum.

- Be understanding and offer lots of support. We know this can be difficult when there are so many other practical and emotional demands draining your time and energy, but there are a number of agencies that can help you support your children. Talk to your doctor or health visitor and call some of the support groups listed in Part 6 of this book.

- Spend quality time with them. Again, this can be difficult when your mind is focused on other worries and concerns, but even a little quality time is better than nothing. Read a book together at bedtime, have dinner at the table together as a family or snuggle up on the sofa and sing songs or watch a film. Your children will appreciate it and it will help strengthen the bond between you.

17

Future relationships

When you leave an abusive relationship, it can take a long time to recover and put your trust in someone again, but at some point in the future you may start to think about meeting someone new. When all the grief, pain and loss is out of the way, you may miss having someone to share your day with and a companion to snuggle up to at night, but naturally you will also be wary about getting involved in case they too become violent.

If a new relationship is the last thing on your mind and you desperately crave peace and quiet for you and your children, trust your instincts and spend time nurturing your own interests and enjoying your new-found freedom. Spending time alone after a difficult relationship is one of the most crucial things you can do for your personal growth and happiness. Take as much time as you need to get to know yourself again. There is no law saying you have to be in a relationship. Some people choose to live life alone and they are among the happiest and most contented people around.

Treat yourself gently and don't rush the healing process. Only when you know and love yourself fully, and have good self-esteem, will you have the strength, energy and confidence to commit to making another relationship work. It isn't fair to get involved with someone when you're carrying around emotional baggage from a previous relationship. Have plenty of counselling and spend quality time on your own, and with your children, and concentrate on making new friends. One day, probably when you least expect it, a lovely person may walk into your life and you will hopefully have recovered enough to welcome him or her, both physically and emotionally.

There are advantages to being in a relationship, but there are also advantages to being single. Relish the time you spend alone, join new activities and start to rebuild your social life, and when you do meet someone new, don't be tempted to introduce him or her to your children too soon. They have suffered a horrible experience and it's possible they may take longer to recover than you. They may also have anxieties or be experiencing things that they haven't told you about, such as a fear of men, flashbacks and nightmares. Introducing a new person into their lives too early in the recovery process could set them back and create added problems. For the time being, give your children your full attention and when you do meet someone new, continue to make the children your number one priority.

You will naturally want some guarantees that what you endured is not going to come back to haunt you in another relationship. Thankfully, since you've already been through it once, in future relationships you will know the warning signs to look for.

Here is a list of the most obvious early warning signs:

- He rushes things – proposes marriage or moves in within days or weeks of meeting.

- He has a history of violence and abuse in past relationships and may be abusive towards his own mother.

- He teases you in a hurtful way in private or in public.

- He says his jealousy is a sign of his love for you.

- He puts you down, either subtly or directly, and undermines your confidence.

- He's very dependent on you for all his needs and may even say 'If you love me, I'm all you need.'

- He is cruel, stand-offish or cold towards your children.

- He doesn't have many friends and shows no interest in making them.

- He is cruel to animals.

- He checks your phone for text messages, new numbers and voicemails.

- He insists on knowing who you're talking to on the phone.

- He gets angry and upset when you're late back from work, shopping or out with friends.

- He talks about moving to the country and living without a phone, car or contact with other people.

- He causes trouble or tries to come between you and your friends. He may suggest that they fancy him or have said things that aren't true.

- He's constantly checking up on you by calling, turning up uninvited and sending other people to check up on you.

- He reads your mail and goes through your handbag and purse.

- He doesn't like you spending time with friends and family.

- He drives dangerously, punches walls or does other things to scare you.

- He accuses you of fancying someone else or being unfaithful.

- He loses his temper easily and without warning.

- He blames you for his problems or bad mood.

- He forces you to have sex when you don't want to.

- He threatens to hurt you, your children, family, friends or pets if you don't do what he wants.

- He stops you from going to work or finding a job.

- He has an alcohol or drug problem and insists that you drink and do drugs with him.

- He is jealous of your friends, family, work, hobbies, children or pets.

- He wants you to spend all of your time with him.

- He says he will kill himself or you if you ever leave.

- He calls you horrible names.

- He checks the mileage on your car.

- He believes women should stay at home and serve men.

- He is verbally abusive and may even push you against a wall and shout right in your face.

- He stops you from using the car, keeps you short of money, gets you into debt, is secretive about money, demands receipts for everything and insists you account for every penny you spend.

However, not everyone shows the same signs, and some people's behaviour might be more extreme than others. Look for subtle warning signs as well as more obvious ones. Sometimes an abuser displays only a couple of warning signs but they are very serious, such as extreme jealousy, temper tantrums over petty things and cruelty to your children or animals. He may act like a spoiled brat if he doesn't get his own way or sulk for hours. Sometimes he may refuse to talk to you for days for something that you've supposedly done that is perfectly innocent.

Above all, trust your instincts. If a situation feels uncomfortable or you strongly suspect it could turn violent, don't wait around to find out. The longer you stay, the more likely you'll be brainwashed and manipulated, and before you know it you'll be back to square one – only this time with a different man.

18

Rebuilding your confidence

Your confidence is one of the first things to go when you are being abused. Fortunately there are ways to get it back. Look at the suggestions on the next few pages which will help you to boost your self-esteem and to begin to feel good about yourself again.

- Make a list of your strong points – write down everything that you're good at and read the list back to yourself regularly. Include big and small things such as being a good mum, making a decent cup of tea, being a good listener, having neat handwriting, being able to change a plug – everything that comes to mind, regardless of how silly it seems!

- Steer clear of negative thoughts and talk to yourself in a positive way. Tell yourself daily that you're a fabulous person who deserves the best. Repeat it often enough and your subconscious will eventually believe it and act accordingly.

- Choose an area of your life that you're good at and want to work at improving even more. Aim to become an expert at it. If you're a good cook, strive to become an even better cook. If you like gardening and are good at it, borrow some gardening books from the library and aim to become an expert. If you enjoy writing poetry or short stories, buy yourself a notebook – a cheap jotter or even scraps of old paper will do – and write whenever you get a few minutes to yourself.

- Visualize yourself as a self-confident person and you will eventually become that person. Whatever we think about most usually happens, so don't be afraid to dream big!

- Surround yourself with positive, confident and successful people. It will help you to look at yourself in a different way and inspire you to become like them.

- Pamper yourself daily with warm baths and healthy food. Style your hair and dress as if you're going somewhere special even if it's just to the shop for a pint of milk! Make that extra effort to look and feel good but do it for yourself and nobody else. Treat yourself like a princess and you will eventually start feeling like one!

- Celebrate your new life – invite old friends around, put some music on and dance! Or dance by yourself or with your children! Dancing, exercise and singing release feel-good hormones that will give your self-esteem a much needed boost.

- Do what you can to make new friends – join in new activities, get involved in the community, volunteer your services, join a mums and toddlers group or chat to other parents at the school gate, and remember to make sure the people you choose to befriend are positive and cheerful!

• Do one thing that you enjoy each day. You don't have to complete the task. Just do one small thing to start moving forward.

Relaxation techniques

Relaxation techniques can be helpful for coping with stress and difficult situations. Done properly, they can help keep you calm in stressful situations and lessen the risk of a panic attack.

Here are some techniques to help you relax that you can start practising today:

• Starting with the muscles in your toes and finishing with your neck and face, tighten each muscle in turn, count to five and then slowly release.

- Close your eyes and focus on your breathing and the sound of your heartbeat. Take a deep breath in through your nose, hold for a count of three, and then breathe out slowly through your mouth. Repeat this several times.

- Close your eyes and picture a peaceful place in your head. Focus on how it makes you feel, and imagine the sights, smells and sounds. Make it as colourful as you like. This is your special place. You can close your eyes and go there whenever you are feeling tense, stressed or scared.

- Smile! Laughing and smiling instantly makes you feel good, regardless of how tense or stressed the people around you are. Next time you are feeling down, exhausted, weak, angry or tense, try smiling or laughing for no reason. As silly as it may sound, it will help!

Positive affirmations

If you've never heard of a positive affirmation before, it's a statement that you say in the present tense to yourself that will ultimately change the way you think and feel. If you repeat positive statements to yourself often enough, you will start to notice big changes in your life and close relationships. You will become a much more positive and assertive person. You may even notice that your abuser changes too, although he probably won't realize it.

What you choose to believe about yourself and the thoughts you choose to think determine your reality. Start today by thinking positive thoughts of health, hope, joy and peace, and while you're at it, paint a picture in your head of the life you wish to lead, and the type of relationship you'd like to have. Be generous with the details and add lots of colour. Now hold that scene and keep picturing it every day as you begin to make it reality.

Here are some things to repeat on a daily basis. It doesn't matter if you say them out loud or in your head – they will have the same effect. Whenever you feel a negative, stressful thought creep up on you, push it away and replace it with a positive thought:

- I am now discovering the new, assertive me.

- I make wise choices and have good judgement.

- I am calm, relaxed and peaceful.

- I am in charge of my life and make wise decisions.

- I am free to do as I please.

- I love and accept myself completely.

- My thoughts and feelings are important.

- I trust my instincts and always act accordingly.

- I am taking responsibility for my family's well-being.

- I am attracting healthy, loving relationships.

- I only spend time with people who are caring and supportive.

- I am open and honest about my experiences to others.

19

Helping someone who is being abused

If you think someone you know is being abused there are many things you can do to help. The most important thing to remember is to prioritize you and your friend's safety above everything else. Approach your friend or relative sensitively and hold back from telling her what to do unless she is in immediate danger. You don't have to know all the answers. What she really needs is to feel less isolated and alone. Having you to lean on and talk to when she is feeling down will help her far more than any direct advice. Tell your friend or relative that you are there for them, and will support them no matter what they decide to do, but also point out the dangers involved and long-term effects of staying in a violent relationship. Make it clear that all abuse is wrong and that none of it is her fault.

You can:

- Stay in regular contact.

- Explore options together.

- Ask how she wants to be supported.

- Pay attention to what she is saying and listen more than you speak.

- Give her plenty of time and space to talk, and be sympathetic, sensitive, understanding and non-judgemental.

- Suggest counselling and support groups available in the area.

- Encourage her to keep a record of the abuse, with dates and times, and offer to take photographs of injuries. Point out that the evidence will come in handy for any future case.

- Explain why you're worried and let her know you want to help.

- Encourage her to make wise decisions and respect the choice she makes.

- Offer to keep copies of important documents and other items she will need if she has to leave home in a hurry.

- Make a list of important numbers, including the number for the National Domestic Violence Helpline (0808 2000 247), Woman's Aid, Refuge, a solicitor, the local police, the local Citizens Advice Bureau and the Rights of Women helpline (see Part 6). Tell your friend to keep the list somewhere safe where it can be found easily.

- Let her know that your door is always open and that she and her children can come and stay with you any time.

- Agree a code word that lets you know she needs help immediately.

- Build her self-esteem, praise her for positive steps she takes and point out her good points.

> *MYTH: Men have a right to discipline their partners.*
>
> **FACT:** Women are not the property of men and they have no right to treat them as such. Domestic violence is a crime and therefore punishable by law.

If you suspect a child or teenager is being abused:

- Approach the subject sensitively.

- Point out your concerns in a gentle way to the child's or teenager's mother or main carer.

- Ask if there is anything you can do to help, such as have the child or teenager stay with you until things at home calm down.

- If nothing changes, and you still suspect abuse, you will need to call social services so that they can assess the situation and offer support. Abuse towards children is a protection issue and will need to be dealt with by the right people to safeguard the welfare of the people involved.

- If a child confides in you, keep talking to her, and more important, keep listening. Spend quality time together and let her know that you believe her and will do everything you can to help. Tell her that the abuse isn't her fault and that she isn't a bad person. Point out that all abuse is wrong. Offer praise and lots of hugs, and don't force her to talk if she doesn't want to. She will open up when she's ready.

- Give her space and time to talk, and be extra patient.

As a friend or relative your support is crucial. There are many ways in which you can help, but the most effective is to be there as a constant and unconditional listening ear. Offer lots of practical help such as babysitting and never tell your friend what to do unless she is in immediate danger. Instead, help her to see that what her abuser is doing is wrong and let her know that there is help available and where she can find it. Above all, be a good friend and be there for her no matter what. With lots of kind and loving support, your friend will eventually come through her experience a much wiser and stronger person. She may not say so, but your friendship and support will make a huge difference to how she feels.

Part 5:
Real Lives

In this section, you will find real stories of violent relationships. Hearing and reading true stories of others who have survived violence and abuse is an inspiration, and simply knowing you are not alone can be a real comfort. Being alone with your problems is very hard, and it helps to know that someone else has been there. It takes courage to admit that you're being abused – it's not an easy thing to do, but the people on the following pages have done just that and so can you.

This section will help you to see that you are not alone, but it will also show you that domestic abuse has no barriers – it can happen to anyone, from anywhere, young and old, male or female. The following stories demonstrate that people who suffer domestic violence are ordinary people from all walks of life with much more in common than the abuse itself – they all suffer the same devastating feelings of hopelessness, confusion and fear every day, but with help and loving support they can move on to happier times.

In Part 5 you will find:

- From the postbag: a series of questions and answers

- Your stories of domestic abuse

- Messages of hope: inspirational advice for victims from fellow sufferers, charities and celebrities.

20

From the postbag

Letters to *This Morning* are never disclosed to anyone, but these created letters are typical of the hundreds that are received each week.

Dear Denise,

I am 21. My mum and dad had a violent marriage (with my mum mainly being violent towards my dad) and my mum used to hit me too. I moved in with my dad when they split up but recently things became difficult with him and so I decided to go and stay with my mum for a while. At first things were going great and then she started using the old abusive ways she had when I was a child. She started using me as a punchbag but I was so scared I couldn't do anything. It took me back to when I was a child, as if it were yesterday. I started to feel as if I needed to be punished for all the naughty things I have done in my childhood. My parents used to tell me I was 'a terrible and evil mistake'. My mum said that 'nasty little girls like you need to be punished.' I began to think she was right and that's why I'm being punished still. I deserve it. I'll be 22 soon and I know I should be happy but I have no one to talk to other than my old teddy. I feel like I have never been allowed to grow up. I know I would be better off dead but I don't even have the courage to do that.

Dear X,

I was so sorry to hear how things are for you at the moment. It must have been devastating when your mum began attacking you soon after you moved back with her. No wonder it took you back to the trauma of your childhood and having flashbacks of those times. It must have been deeply frightening for you.

However, you mustn't allow your mother's wrong actions to affect some of the beliefs that you have about yourself. You are not being punished for 'all the naughty things' you may have done in your childhood. All children misbehave a little and sometimes they need to be checked, but no children are 'terrible and evil'. You are certainly not and the abuse you have suffered is down to your mother and no one else. You don't 'deserve' to be abused, nobody does, and I am sure that if you knew this had happened to a friend of yours you would be telling her the same thing I am telling you now.

In my long experience, trying to 'forget' a traumatic past and put it to the back of your mind simply doesn't work. In order for you to overcome the pain of your past and present (and believe me, you can), you need help from someone who understands. By talking about your experiences, making sense of them and learning that none of this is your fault, you will begin to see things more clearly and work out how to make your life much better. I don't pretend that counselling isn't difficult – talking about traumatic experiences is inevitably painful, but if you can learn to trust your counsellor and the process then you will start to recover. The sooner you do this, the better, and if you talk to your doctor he or she can arrange for you to have some counselling.

I would also urge you to contact either Careline (08457 1228 622) and/or the National Domestic Violence Helpline (0808 2000 247) and talk this through. Don't delay in getting the help you badly need at the moment. I promise you that you won't always feel this way. I know many young women who have been through something very similar to you and they would tell you that it doesn't have to be like this. You are entitled to be happy.

In the meantime, in those dark lonely moments that you feel might overwhelm you, think of me thinking of you and giving you a great big hug.

Dear Denise,

I am 18 years old. Ever since I can remember my dad has been violent. He's not an alcoholic but he does drink a lot and when he does he gets really aggressive. He's beaten me and my sister up for really stupid things but mostly he hits my mum. It was only recently that I found out that my mum had many a beating that I didn't know about. I think she's tried to hide it from us. Me and my sister have tried so many times to get my mum to leave him but she won't. My sister moved out first and then I left. Now I live with my boyfriend. I feel really sorry for my mum as nobody should have to go through that but I hate her for putting herself and me and my sister through all those years of violence and not doing anything to stop it. I want to help her and I'm really worried that one day I'll find out that he's killed her. I cry all the time and sometimes I'm really horrible to my boyfriend. What if I turn into a bully like my dad? And how can I help my mum?

Dear X,

I was so sorry to read about the problems you've been having. You've had to witness and endure a horrendous amount of violence in your life so far and my heart goes out to you. Your house must have been a terrifying place to grow up in, not knowing when your father would become violent next or what he would do. I think you were exceptionally brave to have left but I can quite understand the feelings that it has left you with now that you are outside the situation, on your own and with time to think about what has happened. I can also appreciate the confused feelings you have towards your mother: on the one hand you feel angry for her staying with your father and for not protecting you when you were growing up; on the other you feel frightened for her staying with him when you are powerless to help.

Your mother's decision to stay with him is her decision – she is responsible for determining what she does with her life. You cannot make her change her mind and it is not your job to have to protect her. All you can do is let her know that you love and care about her and will help if ever she wants to get away. After that, try to make sure that you look after yourself. With this in mind, I would suggest that you think about seeking some outside support. It sounds as if all these feelings might be affecting the relationships you share with others in your life. Like many of us, you've probably tried to push bad memories to the back of your mind in the hope that that's where they'll stay. But I expect you've discovered that all too often something triggers the memory and all those painful emotions come flooding back. My concern is that until you have the opportunity to process all that's happened, those residual fears and that anger and confusion will prevent you from really moving forward. I know it takes a leap of faith to trust your feelings to a stranger but if you can find that little bit of courage then you may be able to start putting some of your ghosts to rest and begin moving towards a better and brighter future.

There are various ways to find a counsellor. First, you may like to speak to your doctor and explain the problems you've had to see if he or she could refer you to someone who works within the health service. If your local practice is large enough, they may have their own counsellor. Second, I would recommend that you contact the National Domestic Violence Helpline

(0808 2000 247), which will give you details of counselling services in your area that support anyone who is experiencing or has experienced domestic abuse. You have most of your life ahead of you and I am sure it will be filled with more happiness than you have experienced up to now.

MESSAGE OF HOPE

For too long this has been a hidden crime. We must face up to it and bring it out into the open.

Christina Aguilera

Dear Denise,

I was a single parent when I met my husband. He moved into my house fairly soon afterwards. I became a regular victim of domestic violence after that. I became so scared of my husband and how he would react if I went against his opinions. He used to hit me for the slightest thing, and if he couldn't think of a reason he would still hit me anyway. My husband didn't like me having any communication with my family. He even used to monitor my phone calls. I stayed with him for eight years. My daughter, who was seven at the time, was taken into care following physical abuse by my husband.

I left my husband two years ago and since then I have been trying to build bridges with my family. The only communication I am allowed with my little girl is letters. I have written to my family to explain that I'm no longer married and am getting a divorce, but all they want to know is how I could let my daughter get hurt and be taken into care. They don't understand that there was nothing I could do about it. I would dearly love to have them back in my life but they refuse to talk to me. How can I get my family back?

Dear X,

I was very sorry to read about the difficulties you've been having. It must be very distressing for you to be estranged from your family and your daughter, and my heart goes out to you.

Unfortunately, it isn't uncommon for the family of someone who has been abused over a long period of time to react in this way. Initially, they are sympathetic and concerned, but as time goes on this can turn to frustration as they struggle to understand why their loved one would stay in a violent relationship, especially where there are children. Away from the situation it can seem very black and white, but I understand that when you are living in the middle of an abusive environment day after day, isolated from others, it can seem very different. Abusive partners are very good at making their partners believe that they wouldn't be able to survive in the outside world. Perhaps your partner threatened to really hurt you or your daughter if you left, or prevented you from leaving by keeping you short of money. Whatever the circumstances, you are not alone in having found that it took some time and a great deal of courage to leave.

Have you tried writing to your family and explaining the reasons why it took you this long to leave? If they understand that you have done everything you can to try to repair the damage that has been caused to you and your child then they may feel more ready to welcome you back. I would stress in a letter that you appreciate why your family feel that you let your daughter down and their confusion as to why you didn't escape earlier. In response I would try to explain how you had come to feel in the relationship and how frightened and isolated you were. Give them the time to come around – they may need that, just in the same way as you needed time to find the courage to leave your relationship.

Have you been able to talk this through with anyone? Can I suggest that you perhaps talk it over with the Women and Girls network (0207 610 4345) who offer telephone support to anyone overcoming the experiences of domestic violence. I am sure they will have come across your difficult family situation many times before and may have some helpful and/or reassuring suggestions. I hope that before too long you will be reunited with your daughter and together you can begin to rebuild your life.

Dear Denise,

My friend is 39. I've known her since we were 17 and worked together. She has two daughters. She has made some bad decisions regarding her finances and men, and currently lives with one of her daughters.

A few years ago she met a man who is a bit younger than her and had already spent some time in prison for being violent towards an ex-girlfriend. The relationship is incredibly volatile and he has hit her too. A few months ago he almost kicked her to death. The police said it was one of the worst cases of domestic violence they had ever seen. Despite this, he has continued to live in the house while she has moved out.

The police said they would press charges even though my friend didn't want to. She continued to see him even though he is not supposed to go anywhere near her. She refused to give evidence and he got off! She is moving back with him next week. Her children and family are distraught.

I don't know what to feel. She tells me she loves him and can't live without him and firmly believes he'll never do it again. I know nothing about domestic violence. Is she doing the right thing? I simply can't understand how a woman can return to a man who beat her up so badly. What can I say to her? How can I help?

Dear X,

I entirely understand your difficulty in understanding why your friend could keep forgiving a man who has systematically abused her. When asked the question, many other mistreated women reply as she has – that it is 'because I love him', but this again poses another question – 'why?' You mention that she has made bad decisions about men in the past. I wonder what her family background was. Was it dysfunctional, or did she suffer some early relationship trauma? However, I have known women who grew up in 'normal' homes, but at a young age found themselves in an unhealthy relationship, so perhaps there was no prior reason for her to accept such abuse.

Once someone has had their confidence eroded, been betrayed or abused, it can begin a cycle that can be hard to break. My sense is that she perhaps hasn't learned how to differentiate between a good relationship and a bad one and perhaps has even grown up to believe she is not worth better treatment. Perhaps, too, her partner has repeatedly drummed into her that she couldn't survive without him, or worse that he would come after her if she tried to leave him. If she is in fear of what he may do, then trying to convince herself that she loves him is perhaps the only way she can justify her decision to go back.

It's encouraging that she is still in contact with you. Abusers usually find a way of isolating their partners from family and friends so that they can retain complete control. You can also find that families eventually tire of supporting the abused person and this isolates them further. It's wonderful that you haven't done this, and your support may be key to her recovery.

Hard though it is, try to avoid judging your friend or advising her about what to do. Victims of domestic violence often lose the ability to make positive decisions, and instead slide deeper down the path of abuse rather than face the challenges of leaving. If you can keep listening, and very gently trying to persuade her to seek professional help, then she does have a chance of getting out of this relationship for good.

If you feel she wouldn't feel threatened then you might ask her some questions. For example – what does she see love as being? Love is shown through actions, rather than simply words, and so do his actions seem loving? And when she says 'She couldn't live without him' what does she mean? I wonder whether she literally fears for her life if she were to leave, and she may admit this if asked. Don't force the issues, but if you feel the time is right, then try. You seem a very sensible woman and she must clearly trust you, so I don't doubt you can find the right words.

Finally, I would suggest that you speak to the National Domestic Violence Helpline (0808 2000 247). They will advise you on the best way to support her and hopefully she might be encouraged to speak to them knowing that you have found them helpful. She is very lucky to have you and I sincerely hope that with your help she manages to find the courage to make the bravest and best decision.

MESSAGE OF HOPE

Beating your wife or partner is never acceptable and should not be tolerated. It has no place in civilised society.

Jacqueline Gold

21

Your stories

*Looking back I can't believe why
I went back again and again.*

*I'm afraid to care about anyone now
because that's what makes you believe
the lies and promises that it will never
happen again. Looking back, I can't
understand why I went back again and
again even when I'd managed to make a
new start. Yes, I did love her but it was
more than that. It was a kind of feeling
that if I couldn't make her change
towards me I was a failure as a man.
Now I know she was the failure, but
there's still a fear in me that I could get
into that situation again. I'm very
careful about relationships now but I
still hope to meet someone one day. I'll
be very careful though. Being in hell
once is more than enough.*

David

For a long time, I didn't tell anybody because I thought they wouldn't believe me.

I had such a childish idea of what marriage would be like and he was so lovely when we were courting I thought it would be like that forever. But it was as though a door closed the moment I signed on the dotted line. He told me on our honeymoon how it would be, his word would be law. But even then I never thought he would be violent. I mean, outside he was the perfect husband, everybody's friend. For a long time I didn't tell anybody because I thought they wouldn't believe me. And sometimes I even wondered if I was imagining it. How could that man chatting away so nicely be the man who jammed my fingers in a drawer because I answered back? And the lies trap you because you cover up in the beginning and then you can't undo it so it's more lies. The relief when I rang the number and could tell the truth was the nicest thing that has ever happened to me.

I can talk about it now but I try not to look back too much. I want to move on, for the kids as much as for myself.

Helen

MESSAGE OF HOPE

Going into the refuge was the best decision I ever made. Although I was worried about the children, the services are fantastic. They organize trips to the park and the beach as well as dealing with everything from schools to contact issues. I cannot thank them enough for what they did for us.

Sophia (from the Women's Aid website)

It was cramped in the refuge but I felt really safe.

The thing that hurts me most is what it did to my mam and dad. I was their only child and since I had Rachel I realize what it must have been like for them, watching me suffer. They came to the hospital once when I was in casualty and my dad said, 'He did this, didn't he?' I said no because I was frightened of what he might do if I said yes but I know he didn't believe me. It wasn't until dad was threatened by a heart problem that I got the courage to get out. That and the fact that I could see my daughter go quiet when he was about to kick off. It was as though she knew what was coming. Kids do sense things, don't they? I couldn't go home to my parents because I knew he'd go straight there. It was cramped in the refuge but I felt really safe. You don't realize how tense you've been until you relax and it's as though the temperature's gone up. You just unwind. I'm not frightened of him now because he knows the law is on

my side. I just feel sorry for the next
woman he takes up with though – and
there will be one. He should carry a
government health warning.

Alexia

MESSAGE OF HOPE

I have left the Refuge house to move into
my new flat, a place I hope he will never
find me. Nothing will change what
happened to me but I know that with time
I can learn to live again. My life is getting
better every day and I know I've done the
right thing.

Janet (from the Refuge website)

I want to leave him because I know what staying is doing to me.

I'm writing this at 4 a.m. My daughter is running a temperature and it's just easier to stay up than keep getting in and out of bed to 'that bloody child' as he calls her. I want to leave him because I know what staying is doing to me but, pig that he is, he's a good provider. I don't see how I can give the same standard of living to the kids if I go, even if he let me take them, which he says he would never do. He'd kill me first. I try not to think about the future. If I can just stick it out till they are up and out into the world. After that I don't care what happens. I'm just too tired to care.

Olamide

I couldn't see any way out of it.

I used to listen to you when you said no one should put up with domestic violence. One time you said, 'It doesn't have to be like this' and you looked right into the camera and it felt as though you were saying it to me. But I couldn't see any way out of it. The money thing and where would we go and what would he do because he wouldn't just let it happen. My sister said I could go to her but she has three kids sharing a bedroom already so where would she put my lot? One day I did copy down the number that came up on the screen. I put it away and just having it made me feel better. And then the doctor asked me about the bruises. I was there for a smear test but she asked me to take my coat off and they were there. It was almost like she expected to find them. I made some excuses but I knew she didn't believe me. I felt ashamed on the way home because I could see she pitied me and I used to be quite proud once. I rang the number

*before I took my coat off because I knew
I wouldn't do it otherwise. It just all
happened after that. They didn't push
me, just told me the possibilities. It took
a week and I used to lie in bed
wondering what it would be like not to
have him there snoring his head off or
pushing his beery breath on me. I did
everything they said and it was a lot
easier than I expected. We're happier
now. I still wonder if I was just unlucky
or did I pick a wrong'un, not that it
matters because either way I'm well rid.*

Frankie

MESSAGE OF HOPE

Thousands of women and children are
living in constant fear. For their sakes,
let's not ignore this any longer.

Denise Van Outen

MESSAGE OF HOPE

I'm only 15 years old but I've been abused all my life. I hope you are able to realize that it's not your fault that these things happen, and that you can talk to someone about the abuse today.

Lewis

MESSAGE OF HOPE

I have a choice. I can focus on my parents' abuse and their failure to demonstrate their love to me during the early years of my life. Or I can focus on the good, loving, caring people in my life. I have chosen to focus on the good.

Karen

Part 6:
More Help
at Hand

In this last section, we pull together various sources of help, advice and support and list them in an easy-to-read format to enable you to access professional, emotional and practical guidance quickly and easily. We hope that having a list of useful contact details handy will make you feel less alone, and more supported. There are useful numbers, email and website addresses for organizations that you can turn to in an emergency, along with the contact details of support groups and helplines for children and young victims of domestic violence, elderly victims, male sufferers and gay and lesbian victims. If you are a friend, relative or carer of someone experiencing domestic violence, you will also find useful contacts on these pages. Remember that you can call the 24-hour freephone National Domestic Violence Helpline for confidential advice and information. Whatever you have experienced, or perhaps are still experiencing, there is light at the end of the tunnel. It is now time to reach out to others.

22

Helpful organizations, books and support groups

Dealing with a crisis

In an emergency call 999 for the emergency services in the UK. If it isn't an emergency but you require police assistance, call your local police station. The number will be in the phone book or call directory enquiries.

Beverley Lewis House is a haven for women with learning disabilities who have suffered from abuse or who are at risk of abuse.
Tel: 020 8522 2000
Email: info@east-living.co.uk

The **Black Association of Women Step Out (BAWSO)** offers advice and support to black women who have experienced or are experiencing domestic violence.
Tel: 029 2043 7390

Childline is a free and confidential 24-hour helpline for children and young people. It offers help and advice on any problem and also has a range of publications on various issues including domestic violence.
Tel: 0800 1111
www.childline.org.uk

The Chinese Information and Advice Centre offers information and support on family issues, domestic violence and immigration.
Tel: 020 7692 3697
www.ciac.co.uk

The **Ease Pet Fostering Service** is for animals of women and children fleeing domestic violence.
Tel: 0778 969 7398

The **Freedom Project** is a pet fostering scheme run by Dogs Trust for survivors of domestic violence.
Tel: 07768 616280

Hidden Hurt is a domestic abuse website with lots of information and support.
www.hiddenhurt.co.uk

Jewish Women's Aid (JWA) offers domestic abuse awareness-raising programmes and help.
Tel: 0800 59 12 03

Kiran – Asian Women's Aid provides safe, temporary accommodation for Asian women and their children escaping domestic violence.
Tel: 020 8558 1986
www.rdlogo.com/cwp/kawa/

MIND is a mental health charity that supports people in distress.
Tel: 0845 766 0163
www.mind.org.uk

The National Association for People Abused in Childhood is a charity providing information and advice to adults who suffered abuse and/or neglect in childhood.
Tel: 0800 085 3330

The combined Woman's Aid and Refuge **National Domestic Violence Helpline** is available 24 hours a day, 365 days a year. Call them if you're feeling anxious, scared or confused about your situation or want advice. They can also arrange emergency safe accommodation if required.
Tel: 0808 2000 247

Call the **National Society for the Prevention of Cruelty to Children (NSPCC)** if you are worried about a child.
Tel: 0808 800 5000; www.nspcc.org.uk

If you or someone you know has been raped, call **The Rape Crisis Foundation** for support and advice.
Tel: 0115 900 3560

Refuge provides support and emergency accommodation for women and children when they need to leave home because of domestic violence.

Tel: Combined Women's Aid and Refuge helpline 0808 2000 247

Email: info@refuge.org.uk

www.refuge.org.uk

Reunite is a support group for parents of children who have been abducted.

Tel: 0116 255 6234

www.reunite.org

If you are in a crisis and live in the UK, you can ring the **Samaritans** at any time of the day or night, 365 days a year.

Tel: 0845 790 9090

Shakti Women's Aid is a voluntary organization based in Edinburgh offering support to black minority ethnic women (over 16 years) and their children experiencing or escaping domestic abuse.

Tel: 0131 475 2399

www.shaktiedinburgh.co.uk

Shelter is a national organization in the UK that helps improve the lives of homeless and badly housed people.
Tel: 0808 800 4444
www.shelter.org.uk

Supportline is a telephone helpline providing confidential emotional support to children, young people and adults on any issue including domestic violence. They keep details of other agencies, support groups and counsellors throughout the UK.
Tel: 020 8554 9004
Email: info@supportline.org.uk

The Tulip Project supports parents who have suffered domestic violence at the hands of their children.
Tel: 0151 637 6363

Victim Support offers information and support to victims of crime, whether or not they have reported the crime to the police.
Tel: 0845 303 0900
www.victimsupport.org

Women's Aid is a national domestic abuse charity that helps women and children. They operate a 24-hour National Domestic Violence Helpline (run in partnership with Refuge).
Helpline: 808 2000 247
General enquiries: 0117 944 44 11
Email helpline@womensaid.org.uk.
www.womensaid.org.uk

The **Irish Women's Aid Domestic Abuse** helpline is available 24 hours a day, seven days a week, 365 days a year.
Tel: 1800 341 900
www.womensaid.ie

The **Scottish Women's Aid Domestic Abuse** helpline is available 24 hours a day, seven days a week, 365 days a year.
Tel: 0800 027 1234
www.scottishwomensaid.co.uk

The **Welsh Women's Aid Domestic Abuse** helpline is available 24 hours a day, seven days a week, 365 days a year.
Tel: 0808 80 10 800
www.welshwomensaid.org

Help for men

AMEN offers a confidential helpline, information and support for male victims and their children in Ireland. It also runs assertiveness courses and support groups and can provide face-to-face counselling if required.

Tel: 00 353 46 90 23718

www.amen.ie

The **Dyn Wales** is a Welsh helpline for male victims of domestic abuse.

Tel: 0808 801 0321

www.dynproject.org

The Male Rape/Sexual Abuse (MRSA) Support Association 24-hour helpline offers help and support to male victims of rape, adult male survivors of childhood sexual abuse and male victims of domestic violence.

Tel: 07932 898274

Email: malerapemrsa@yahoo.co.uk

www.malerapesexualabuse.ik.com

Man to Man provides emotional support, and practical and legal advice on matters like housing and injunctions.

Tel: 020 8698 9649; Email: **grolph@no-more-silence.org**

Mankind offers professional support, information, practical advice and counselling for men who have been sexually abused, sexually assaulted and/or raped.
Tel: 0870 794 4124
www.mankind.org.uk

Men's Advice Line (MALE) offers advice and support for men in abusive relationships.
Tel: 0845 064 6800
Email: info@mensadviceline.org.uk
www.mensadviceline.org.uk

Men's Aid is a charity in Scotland providing emotional and practical support, information and advice, accommodation, and advice on finance and legal issues. It can also help gain and maintain contact with children and provide safe accommodation for men and their children in Scotland at a refuge.
Tel: 01334 474348

Survivors is a helpline for male victims of sexual abuse.
Tel: 020 7357 8299

Victim Support is a male helpline for male victims of domestic violence or sexual abuse.
Tel: 0800 328 3623

Help for children and teenagers

The **British Association of Psychotherapists** offers advice and guidance on psychotherapy for children.
Tel: 020 8452 9823
Email: mail@bap-psychotherapy.org.uk
www.bap-psychotherapy.org.uk

Barnardo's helps children, young people and their families overcome severe disadvantages such as abuse, homelessness and poverty.
www.barnardos.org.uk

Childline is a free and confidential 24-hour helpline for children and young people. It offers help and advice on any problem and also has a range of publications on various issues including domestic violence.
Tel: 0800 1111
www.childline.org.uk

Children 1st is an organization in Scotland that aims to give every child in Scotland a safe and secure childhood.

Tel: 0131 446 2300

www.children1st.org.uk

DABS (Directory and Book Services) sells a national directory listing over 800 organizations in the UK and Ireland related to childhood abuse and child sexual abuse.

Tel: 0117 923 9318

www.dabsbooks.co.uk

The **Eating Disorders Association** offer help with eating disorders.

Tel: 0845 634 1414

www.edauk.com

Eighteen and Under is an organization in Scotland that offers support, information and a helpline to people under 18 who have experienced any type of abuse.

Tel: 0800 731 4080

www.18u.org.uk

Get Connected is a free telephone and email helpline dedicated to finding young people the best help no matter what the problem. It will put a child or young person in touch with a UK helpline where appropriate.

Tel: 0808 808 4994

Email: help@getconnected.org.uk

www.getconnected.org.uk

The **Help with self-harming** site offers information and support for young people who self-harm, their friends and families, and professionals working with them.

www.selfharm.org.uk

The Hideout website for children and young people.

www.thehideout.org.uk

The **National Association of Citizen's Advice Bureau** offers free, confidential, impartial and independent legal advice. To find out the location of your nearest office visit the website.

www.citizensadvice.org.uk

Parentline Plus offers information and support to anyone parenting a child. Parentline Plus runs a freephone helpline and courses for parents.
Tel: 0808 800 2222
www.parentlineplus.org.uk

There 4 Me is a website for 12–16 year olds who are worried about something and need help. There is an online chat facility, message boards, an agony aunt and trained counsellors to talk to in confidence.
www.there4me.com

Worried Need 2 Talk is a website for young people.
www.worriedneed2talk.org.uk

Help for the elderly

Action on Elder Abuse is a charity that aims to prevent abuse in old age.
Tel: 0808 808 8141
Email: enquiries@elderabuse.org.uk
www.elderabuse.org.uk

Help the Aged is committed to ending elder abuse. They offer advice, information and support to victims and their carers.

Tel: 020 7278 1114 (England),
  0131 551 6331 (Scotland),
  02920 346 550 (Wales) or
  02890 230 666 (Northern Ireland).
Email: info@helptheaged.org.uk
www.helptheaged.org.uk

Help for gays and lesbians

Broken Rainbow is a telephone helpline offering advice and support for lesbian, gay, bisexual and transgender victims of domestic violence.
Tel: 08452 60 44 60
www.broken-rainbow.org.uk

The **London Lesbian and Gay Switchboard** offers 24-hour information and support for lesbians and gay men.
Tel: 020 7837 7324; **www.llgs.org.uk**

Survivors of Lesbian Partner Abuse (SOLA) supports women who have experienced domestic violence within a lesbian relationship.
Tel: 020 7328 7389

Moving forward

Divorce Aid provides divorce advice, support and information on any matter concerning you and your divorce. It also offers mediation, counselling and professional legal advice.
Email: office@divorceaid.co.uk
www.divorceaid.co.uk

The Relationships Centre provides a wide variety of support to men, women and young people to help them overcome difficulties in their lives.
Tel: 0800 783 9636.
www.healthyrelationships.org.uk

Gingerbread is an organization for one-parent families, offering advice, support groups and a telephone helpline to single parents.
Tel: 0800 018 4318
www.gingerbread.org.uk

The Women and Girls Network offer telephone support to anyone overcoming the experiences of domestic violence.
Tel: 020 7610 4345

Legal advice

The **Children and Family Court Advisory and Support Service** is an organization that looks after the interests of children involved in family proceedings and advises the courts on what it considers to be their best interests.
Tel: 020 7510 7000
Email: webenquiries@caffcass.gov.uk
www.caffcass.gov.uk

If you are the victim of domestic violence and no longer living with your partner, you may be able to claim compensation through the **Criminal Injuries Compensation Scheme.**
Tel: 020 7842 6800 (London) or
0141 331 2726 (Glasgow)
www.cica.gov.uk

Divorce Aid provides professional legal advice on any matter concerning your divorce. It also offers mediation and counselling.
Email: office@divorceaid.co.uk
www.divorceaid.co.uk

The **National Association of Citizen's Advice Bureaux** offers free, confidential, impartial and independent legal advice. To find out the location of your nearest office visit the website.
www.citizensadvice.org.uk

Rights of Women provides a telephone legal advice service for women, offering advice and information on sexual violence and harassment, employment rights, relationship breakdown and arrangements for children, lesbian parenting, and domestic violence. It also provides referrals to sympathetic women solicitors.
Tel: 020 7251 6577
Email: info@row.org.uk
www.rightsofwomen.org.uk

The **Sexual Violence Legal** helpline offers legal advice on all matters relating to sexual violence.
Tel: 020 7251 8887

Victim Support offers information and support to victims of crime, whether or not they have reported the crime to the police.
Tel: 0845 303 0900
www.victimsupport.org

Helping an abuser

The British Psychological Society will offer information and advice on finding a psychotherapist, psychologist or counsellor in your area.
Tel: 0116 254 9568
Email: enquiry@bps.org.uk
www.bps.org.uk

The **Everyman Project** is a UK national helpline for anyone concerned about violence. It provides a counselling service for violent men who want to change.
Tel: 020 7263 8884
Email: everymanproject@btopenworld.com
www.everymanproject.co.uk

The **Freedom Programme** is a 12-week programme for any man who wishes to stop abusing women and children.
Tel: 0151 630 0651
Email: atcraven@aol.com
www.freedomprogramme.co.uk

The Mankind Initiative provides treatment for female abusers.
Tel: 0870 794 4124
www.mankind.org.uk

Respect is a helpline providing information and advice for perpetrators of domestic violence. It also offers a domestic violence abuser support programme.
Tel: 0845 122 8609
Email: info@respect.uk.net
www.respect.uk.net

Finding a counsellor

Counselling is free on the UK national health service so if you would like to speak to a counsellor, ask your GP or health visitor to arrange a referral. Alternatively, you can call the **British Association for Counselling and Psychotherapy** for details of local counsellors, most of whom charge a fee for their services.
Tel: 0870 443 5252
www.bacp.co.uk

The British Psychological Society will offer information and advice on finding a psychotherapist, psychologist or counsellor in your area.
Tel: 0116 254 9568
Email: enquiry@bps.org.uk
www.bps.org.uk

The **British Association of Psychotherapists** offers advice and guidance on psychotherapy for children.
Tel: 020 8452 9823
Email: mail@bap-psychotherapy.org.uk
www.bap-psychotherapy.org.uk

Further reading

Behind Closed Doors, Jenny Tomlin, Hodder &
    Stoughton, 2006

Breaking The Chains of Abuse: A Practical Guide,
    Sue Atkinson, Lion Hudson, 2006

*Breaking the Cycle of Abuse: How to Move Beyond
    Your Past to Create an Abuse-free Future*,
    Beverley Engel, John Wiley & Sons, 2005

Childhood Experiences of Domestic Violence,
    Caroline McGee, Jessica Kingsley Publishers,
    2000

*Controlling People: How to Recognize, Understand
    and Deal with People Who Try to Control You*,
    Patricia Evans, Adams Media Corporation,
    2002

Cry Salty Tears, Dinah O' Dowd, Century, 2007

*Family & Friends' Guide to Domestic Violence: How
    to Listen, Talk and Take Action When Someone
    You Care About Is Being Abused*, Elaine Weiss,
    Valcano Press, 2004

*Friday's Child: What Has She Done That Is So
    Terrible?*, Sandra Crossley, Mandarin Press, 2004

*Getting Out: Life Stories of Women Who Left
    Abusive Men*, Ann Goetting, Vision, 2000

Hitting and Hurting: Living in a Violent Family,
    Fran Pickering, Children's Society, 2000

How Long Does it Hurt? A Guide to Recovering from Incest and Sexual Abuse for Teenagers, their Friends, and their Families, Mather, Jossey Bass Wiley, 2004

How to Break Your Addiction to a Person, Howard M. Halpern, Bantam, 1982

In Fear of Her Life: The True Story of a Violent Marriage, Frances Smith & Erin McCafferty, Maverick House, 2004

In Sheep's Clothing: Understanding and Dealing with Manipulative People, George K. Simon, A. J. Christopher and Company, 1996

Infernal Child: World Without Love, Erin Pizzey, Little Hermit Press, 2005

Is Your Parent in Good Hands? Protecting Your Aging Parent From Financial Abuse and Neglect, Edward J. Carnot, Capital Books, 2004

It's My Life Now: Starting Over After an Abusive Relationship or Domestic Violence, Meg Dugan, Routledge, 2000

Living with the Devil, Amy Norman, John Blake Publishing, 2006

Love and Pain: A Survival Handbook for Women, Sandra Horley, Bedford Square Press, 1988

Men Who Are Good For You and Men Who Are Bad, Susanna Hoffman, Ten Speed Press, 1987

Men Who Batter Women, Adam Jukes, Routledge, 1999

No More Secrets for Me: A Book for Adults to Share with Children, Oralee Wachter, Little, Brown & Company, 2002

No More Secrets: Violence in Lesbian Relationships, Janice L. Ristock, Routledge, 2002

Please Daddy, No: A Boy Betrayed, Stuart Howarth, Harper Element, 2006

Power and Control: Why Charming Men Make Dangerous Lovers, Sandra Horley, Vermillion, 2000

Shattered Dreams: One Woman's Escape to Freedom from an Abusive Marriage, Susan Stewart, Mainstream Publishing, 1998

Stop Hitting Mum! Children Talk About Domestic Violence, Audrey Mullender, Young Voice, 2003

Terrifying Love, Lenore E. Walker, Harper and Row, 1989

The Battered Woman, Lenore E. Walker, Harper and Row, 1989

The Courage to Heal: A Guide for Women Survivors of Child Sexual Abuse, Ellen Bass, Vermilion, 2002

The Emotionally Abused Woman: Overcoming Destructive Patterns and Reclaiming Yourself, Beverley Engel, Fawcett Books, 1992

The Manipulative Man: Identify His Behavior, Counter the Abuse, Regain Control, Dorothy McCoy, Adams Media Corporation, 2006

The Secret of Overcoming Verbal Abuse: Getting Off the Emotional Roller Coaster and Regaining Control of Your Life, Albert Ellis and Marcia Grad Powers, Wilshire Book Company, 2000

The Step Child: A True Story, Donna Ford, Vermilion, 2006

The Verbally Abusive Man, Can He Change? A Woman's Guide to Deciding Whether to Stay or Go, Patricia Evans, Adams Media Corporation, 2006

The Verbally Abusive Relationship: How to Recognize it and How to Respond, Patricia Evans, Adams Media Corporation, 2002

Ugly, Constance Briscoe, Hodder & Stoughton, 2006

Understanding Family Violence: Treating and Preventing Partner, Child, Sibling and Elder Abuse, Vernon R. Wiehe, SAGE Publications, 1998

Violence in Gay and Lesbian Domestic Partnerships,
Claire M. Renzetti and Charles H. Miley,
Harrington Park Press, 1996

Violent No More: Helping Men End Domestic Abuse,
Michael Paymar, Hunter House, 2000

*When Love Goes Wrong: What to Do When You
Can't Do Anything Right*, Ann Jones and Susan
Schechter, Harper Perennial, 1993

Why Do I Think I Am Nothing Without a Man?,
Penelope Russianoff, Bantam, 1984

*Why Does He Do That? Inside The Minds of Angry
and Controlling Men*, Lundy Bancroft, Berkeley
Publishing Group, 2003

Women and Self-esteem, Mary Ellen Donovan and
Linda Tscirhart Sanford, Penguin, 1984

Women Who Love Too Much, Robin Norwood,
Pocket, 1990

Your Body Belongs to You, Cornelia Maud
Spelman, Albert Whitman & Company, 2000

Also available from *This Morning* and Hodder Education are:

- This Morning: Get Over Your Break-up

- This Morning: Get Out of Debt

- This Morning: Beat Your Depression

- This Morning: Cope With Bereavement

- This Morning: Beat Your Addiction

- This Morning: Overcome Your Postnatal Depression

- This Morning: Cope With Infertility